# SMALL INTERIORS
# PETITS INTÉRIEURS
# KLEINE RÄUME

# SMALL INTERIORS
# PETITS INTÉRIEURS
# KLEINE RÄUME

EVERGREEN

EVERGREEN is an imprint of

Taschen GmbH

© 2006 TASCHEN GmbH

Hohenzollernring 53, D-50672 Köln

**www.taschen.com**

Editor  Editrice  Redakteur:
**Simone Schleifer**

English translation  Traduction anglaise  Englische Übersetzung:
**Jane Wintle**

French translation  Traduction française  Französische Übersetzung:
**Marion Westerhoff**

German translation  Traduction allemande  Deutsche Übersetzung:
**Susanne Engler**

Proof reading  Relecture  Korrektur lesen:
**Matthew Clarke, Marie-Pierre Santamarina, Martin Rolshoven**

Art director  Direction artistique  Art Direktor:
**Mireia Casanovas Soley**

Graphic design and layout  Mise en page et maquette  Graphische Gestaltung und Layout:
**Diego González, Elisabet Rodríguez**

Printed by  Imprimé par  Gedruckt durch:
Gráficas Toledo, Spain

ISBN: 3-8228-5139-6

In the early 19th century, the large-scale migration from the country to the cities induced by industrialization gave rise to radical changes in lifestyle; in our times, population growth, largely concentrated in major cities, has led to increasing limitations on the size of homes. At the same time, property developers have realized the great benefits of residential blocks and confined spaces set on small lots. The main reason for the emergence of this type of housing is the rise in property prices, which has prompted many young people to consider the option of living in a small apartment. Furthermore, the increasing scarcity of land suitable for construction considerably reduces the possibilities of accommodating a mushrooming population, unless homes are reduced in size. From a financial point of view, housing costs would be significantly reduced if investment was focused not so much on quantity and size but more on quality. Finally, the squandering of scarce natural resources has given rise to a heightened ecological awareness: large, isolated houses need more energy, consume more resources, occupy a greater expanse of land and produce more waste. This energy output could be minimized if small homes became a commonplace solution in cities with a great population density.

In recent years, the trend toward smaller homes has become not only a necessity but also an alternative lifestyle. Many architects and designers as well as a growing number of buyers who could certainly afford a bigger residence are now opting for a home of limited dimensions, because they have learnt to discover the pleasures and recognize the potential of living in a small space. Nowadays, the new contemporary lifestyle revolves around such spaces, in the form of apartments, duplexes, lofts and houses propitious to countless innovative solutions for reduced dimensions: multifunctional furniture, combined areas, rooms with a double function, built-in closets, movable tables, sliding doors, etc. Moreover, technological advances have enabled once bulky music systems, televisions and lighting equipment to become not only smaller but also more practical and attractive. Other factors such as the appropriate lighting, layout and choice of materials help create the illusion that much more space is available than is really the case. Skylights, spotlights, reflecting surfaces, translucent materials, partitions... the possibilities are infinite.

Full of practical, attractive and inspiring ideas, *Small Interiors* presents a broad selection of homes from all over the world, created by prestigious architects and designers.

Au début du XIXe siècle, la migration massive de la campagne vers la ville liée à l'industrialisation, a changé radicalement le style de vie de la population. Actuellement, la croissance démographique et sa concentration accrue dans les grandes villes ont fait apparaître des habitations aux dimensions toujours plus réduites. En même temps, les promoteurs immobiliers se sont rendus compte des bénéfices potentiels offerts par les immeubles collectifs et par les espaces insérés dans des lieux de plus en plus étroits. L'apparition de ce type de maison est surtout due à l'augmentation du coût de l'habitat, conduisant nombre de jeunes à envisager l'option de vivre dans un petit appartement. En outre, la pénurie de sol constructible réduit considérablement les possibilités de loger une population en constante augmentation, à moins que l'habitat ne se réduise ou devienne plus compact. Sur le plan économique, son coût diminuerait de manière substantielle, si on investissait davantage dans la qualité plus que dans la quantité ou la taille. Par ailleurs, le manque de ressources naturelles et leur exploitation abusive sont à l'origine d'une grande prise de conscience écologique : les grandes maisons individuelles dépensent plus d'énergie, consomment davantage de ressources, occupent une plus grande étendue de terrain et engendrent davantage de déchets. Ce gaspillage d'énergie pourrait diminuer si la solution des petites habitations devenait monnaie courante dans les villes à forte densité de population.

Au cours des dernières années, la tendance en faveur de maisons plus petites et intimes est devenue non seulement une nécessité, mais aussi un mode de vie alternatif. De nombreux architectes et designers ainsi que des acquéreurs, en nombre toujours croissant, qui pourraient sans problèmes acheter une habitation plus grande, optent pour une maison aux dimensions réduites. En définitive, tout un chacun apprend à découvrir le plaisir et à envisager la possibilité d'habiter dans un espace plus petit. A l'heure actuelle, le nouveau style de vie contemporain, créatif et original à souhait, tourne autour de ces espaces, sous forme d'appartements, duplex, lofts et habitations, où il est possible de faire valoir une foule de solutions novatrices pour espaces limités : mobilier aux fonctions multiples, zones polyvalentes, pièces à double fonctions, armoires encastrées, tables portables, portes coulissantes, etc. En outre, de nos jours, les progrès de la technologie ont permis de réduire considérablement la taille des anciens appareils encombrants de musique, télévision et d'installations d'éclairage. D'autres facteurs, créant l'illusion de disposer d'un espace plus grand qu'en réalité, entrent en jeux, à l'instar de la distribution et du choix de matériaux : lucarnes, puits de lumière, surfaces réfléchissantes, matériaux translucides, partitions… les possibilités sont infinies.

Une foule d'idées pratiques, attractives et inspiratrices à la clé, *Petits intérieurs* présente une ample sélection d'habitations du monde entier, conçues par des architectes et designers de renom.

Zu Beginn des 19. Jh. änderte sich bedingt durch die massive Migration vom Land in die Städte der Lebensstil der Bevölkerung auf radikale Weise. Diese Veränderungen haben zu einer Situation geführt, in der immer mehr Menschen in den Städten auf kleinstem Raum leben, so dass auch die Wohnungen immer kleiner werden. Gleichzeitig hat man im Immobiliensektor bemerkt, welche potentiellen Gewinne Mehrfamilienhäuser und kleine Räumlichkeiten in immer enger werdenden Umgebungen versprechen. Der Trend zu diesem Wohnungstyp ist vor allem auf die hohen Immobilienpreise zurückzuführen, die viele junge Leute dazu zwingen, in einer kleinen Wohnung zu leben. Außerdem mangelt es an Bauland, so dass man die ständig wachsende Bevölkerung nicht ausreichend mit Wohnraum versorgen kann, es sei denn, die Wohnungen werden kleiner und kompakter. Vom wirtschaftlichen Standpunkt aus gesehen würden die Wohnungspreise erheblich fallen, wenn man anstatt in Größe mehr in Qualität investieren würde. Zu dieser ganzen Situation kommt noch hinzu, dass aufgrund des Mangels an natürlichen Rohstoffen auch das ökologische Gewissen der Bevölkerung sich immer stärker entwickelt. Große und isoliert stehende Häuser verbrauchen mehr Energie und Rohstoffe, sie nehmen ein größeres Gelände ein und erzeugen mehr Abfälle. Die Energiekosten könnten verringert werden, wenn die kleinen Wohnungen zu der üblichen Lösung in Städten mit einer großen Bevölkerungsdichte werden würden.

Während der letzten Jahre ist der Trend zu kleineren und intimeren Räumen nicht nur zu einer Notwendigkeit geworden, sondern auch zu einem alternativen Lebensstil. Zahlreiche Architekten, Innenarchitekten und immer mehr Käufer, die sich sicherlich auch eine größere Wohnung hätten leisten können, entscheiden sich für eine kleine Wohnung. Man hat ganz offensichtlich die Annehmlichkeiten und die Möglichkeiten entdeckt, die eine kleine Wohnumgebung zu bieten hat. Heutzutage dreht sich der zeitgenössische Lebensstil voller Kreativität und Originalität um solche Arten von Wohnungen. Räume, die zu einfachen Wohnungen, zweistöckigen Wohnungen und Lofts werden, in denen man zahlreiche innovative Lösungen für kleine Räume umsetzen kann wie z. B. multifunktionelle Möbel, kombinierte Bereiche, Räume mit einer doppelten Funktion, Einbauschränke, mobile Tische, Schiebetüren usw.. Außerdem hat der technische Fortschritt es möglich gemacht, dass Geräte, die früher riesig waren, wie z. B. Stereoanlagen, Fernseher und Beleuchtungskörper, heute immer kleiner, praktischer und ästhetischer werden. Andere Faktoren, die dazu beitragen, einen Raum größer wirken zu lassen, sind die korrekte Beleuchtung, Verteilung und Materialauswahl. Dachfenster, Scheinwerfer, reflektierende Flächen, lichtdurchlässige Materialien, Raumteiler,.... die Möglichkeiten sind unbegrenzt.

*Kleine Räume* ist voller praktischer, gewagter und inspirierender Ideen und stellt eine große Auswahl an Wohnungen auf der ganzen Welt vor, die von berühmten Architekten und Innenarchitekten entworfen wurden.

# SMALL INTERIORS
## PETITS INTÉRIEURS
## KLEINE RÄUME

# Wee House
## Maison Wee
### Wee Haus

Geoffrey Warner / Alchemy

The basic concept of this project consisted of building a simple, unconventional, and affordable cabin that would be used for occasional retreats by a violinist. The site chosen was a vast plain near Lake Pepin in Minnesota. The small cabin, a 334-sq.-ft cube, contains a studio whose depth is the result of efficient use of space. The bedroom, living area, and kitchen are located on a single level without any interior walls, and are open to the outside thanks to the windows that run along the front and back walls. The wood that covers the floor, ceiling, and sides adds warmth and comfort to the dwelling, while the windows create a spacious feeling in the interior. Despite its Minimalist exterior, the cabin is decisively rustic; without electricity and running water, the only source of heat is the fireplace in the center of the space. This completely prefabricated cabin, whose unique style stems from its simplicity and method of construction, was completed in eight weeks.

Le concept initial était de construire une cabane simple, peu conventionnelle et économique, comme refuge temporaire d'une violoniste. Le lieu choisi est une vaste esplanade proche du lac Pepin, au Minnesota. La cabane, de petites dimensions, un cube de 31 m², a fait l'objet d'une étude approfondie pour optimaliser l'espace. Chambre à coucher, séjour et cuisine sont centrés sur un seul étage dépourvu de subdivisions, ouvert sur l'espace grâce à des parois de verre qui parcourent les façades frontale et dorsale. Le bois sur le sol, le toit et les murs imprègnent le refuge de chaleur et de confort. Les baies vitrées créent une sensation de largesse. Malgré un extérieur minimaliste, la cabane est vraiment rustique : en l'absence d'électricité et d'eau courante, l'unique source de chaleur est une cheminée située au centre du séjour. Simplicité et méthode de construction aidant, cette cabane originale, entièrement préfabriquée, a été achevée en huit semaines.

Der Ausgangspunkt für die Planer war, eine einfache, ausgefallene, aber nicht allzu teure Hütte zu errichten, in die sich der Kunde von Zeit zu Zeit zurückziehen kann. Dazu wurde eine weite Ebene in der Nähe des Sees Pepin in Minnesota ausgewählt. Die Hütte ist ein kleiner, 31 m² großer Würfel, in dem der Platz so effizient genutzt wurde, dass eine geräumige Studiowohnung entstand. In einer einzigen Etage befinden sich das Schlafzimmer, das Wohnzimmer und die Küche. Es gibt keine weiteren Unterteilungen, und die Hütte öffnet sich über die Fenster an der Vorder- und Hinterfassade zur Landschaft. Das Holz des Bodens, der Decke und der Wände schafft eine warme und komfortable Atmosphäre. Obwohl die Hütte von außen recht minimalistisch aussieht, ist sie innen sehr rustikal. Es gibt weder fließendes Wasser noch Strom, und die einzige Wärmequelle ist ein Kamin im Zentrum des Wohnzimmers. Aufgrund dieser Einfachheit und des Konstruktionssystems wurde diese vorgefertigte Hütte in nur acht Wochen errichtet.

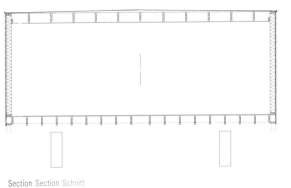

Section Section Schnitt

Elevation Élévation Aufriss

Wooden floors, ceilings and walls give the cabin a warm, comfortable feel, while the large windows convey a sense of space to the interior.

Le bois recouvrant le sol, le toit et les murs confèrent au refuge, chaleur et confort, tandis que les baies vitrées parviennent à créer une sensation d'amplitude à l'intérieur.

Das Holz des Bodens, der Decke und der Wände schafft eine warme und komfortable Atmosphäre, während durch die Fenster der Eindruck von Weite entsteht.

The furniture is placed facing the balconies: both the bed and the hob are by the window, so that the wide open spaces outside can be admired.

Le mobilier est placé face aux balcons : le lit comme la cuisine sont alignés le long des baies vitrées, permettant d'admirer l'immensité du paysage.

Das Mobiliar verteilt sich vor den Balkonen, sowohl das Bett als auch die Küche befinden sich an den Fenstern, so dass man die weite Landschaft bewundern kann.

## ☐ Cabin at Chicken Point
## Cabane à Chicken Point
## Hütte am Chicken Point

Olson Sundberg Kundig Allen Architects

This project involved the construction of a cabin in the middle of the woods, next to a lake, from where the surrounding countryside could be enjoyed. A 9x6 metre window frame was designed to overlook the wooded area. In addition, a window offering views of the lake was provided in the bedroom. The house comprises three basic sections: a concrete volume, a plywood superstructure and a cylindrical aluminium chimney one metre in diameter. Because of its central location in the living room, which is a completely open space, the fireplace warms the whole house, thereby providing an economic benefit as well as an agreeable atmosphere within the woodland setting. Low-maintenance materials, such as concrete, steel and plywood, were left untreated, so that they would age naturally.

Ce projet prévoyait la construction d'une cabane au milieu de la forêt, à côté d'un lac, pour contempler le paysage alentour. A cet effet, les architectes ont conçu une verrière de 9×6 m ouverte sur la nature arborée. De plus, dans la chambre à coucher, une fenêtre de toit, permet de jouir des vues sur le lac. La maison est constituée de trois éléments essentiels : un volume de béton, une insertion de contreplaqué de bois et une cheminée circulaire d'un mètre de diamètre. Au cœur de la salle de séjour, espace entièrement ouvert, la cheminée, qui chauffe toute la maison, est un élément à la fois économique et accueillant dans cet univers boisé. Les matériaux faciles d'entretien, à l'instar du béton, de l'acier et du contreplaqué de bois ne sont pas traités afin de vieillir naturellement.

Es sollte eine Hütte mitten im Wald, direkt an einem See entstehen, von der aus man die Landschaft der Umgebung betrachten kann. Deshalb wurde eine 9 x 6 m große Vitrine konstruiert, die sich zu den Bäumen hin öffnet. Das Schlafzimmer liegt an einem Fenster, von dem aus man auf den See blickt. Das Haus besteht aus drei Grundelementen: einer Form aus Beton, einem Einsatz aus Sperrholz und einem runden Aluminiumkamin mit einem Meter Durchmesser. Der Kamin steht mitten im Wohnzimmer, das ein völlig offener Raum ist, so dass er das ganze Haus heizt und zu einem wirtschaftlichen und gleichzeitig sehr gemütlichen Element in dieser bewaldeten Region wird. Die verwendeten Materialien Beton, Stahl und Sperrholz sind pflegeleicht und unbehandelt, damit sie auf natürliche Weise altern.

Magnificent views of the lake and the surrounding countryside are enjoyed from the living room.

Depuis le salon, les vues sur le lac et le paysage environnant sont magnifiques.

Vom Wohnzimmer aus genießt man den wundervollen Blick auf den See und die umgebende Landschaft.

The house was specially designed to open out onto the surrounding landscape.

La maison est spécialement construite pour s'ouvrir sur l'extérieur et bénéficier au maximum des vues sur le paysage environnant.

Das Haus wurde eigens so gebaut, dass es sich nach außen öffnet und man den Panoramablick auf die Umgebung wirklich genießen kann.

A window offering views of the lake was installed in the bedroom.

Dans la chambre à coucher, une baie vitrée permet d'admirer la vue panoramique sur tout le lac.

Das Schlafzimmer wurde mit einem großen Fenster ausgestattet, das ebenfalls den Blick auf den ganzen See freigibt.

# House on Eel Pie Island
## Maison sur l'île de Eel Pie
## Haus auf der Insel Eel Pie

Boyarsky Murphy Architects

The original building, made from wood and prefabricated panels, was the site of the public baths. Although the location offered a high-quality natural environment, the existing structure was in a bad state of dilapidation. Nevertheless, the concrete foundations and some of the wooden structures were preserved, and they now benefit from a new roof that directs the house toward the river. The roof consists of two juxtaposed inclined planes held above the building by means of small cylindrical columns, anchored or embedded in the walls. The front elevation was replaced by a metal frame, which holds a double-glazed sliding screen. The remaining internal divisions were removed and a new interior arrangement based on walls stopping short of the ceiling allowed the upper window to enhance the perception of spaciousness throughout the house.

L'édifice préexistant qui accueillait des bains publics, était formé d'une ossature de bois et de panneaux préfabriqués. Si les conditions naturelles du site étaient idéales, la structure existante était en très mauvais état. Malgré tout, les fondations de béton et quelques éléments de la structure de bois ont pu être conservés. Aujourd'hui, ils supportent une nouvelle toiture qui oriente la maison vers la rivière. Le toit est formé de deux plans juxtaposés et inclinés flottant au-dessus de l'édifice, soutenus par deux petites colonnes circulaires, ancrées ou encastrées dans les murs. La hauteur de façade a été remplacée par un cadre de métal, soutenant une paroi à double vitrage coulissante. Le reste des partitions a été éliminé et la nouvelle distribution repose sur des murs qui ne vont pas jusqu'au plafond, accentuant la fluidité de la fenêtre supérieure et permettant de percevoir l'espace total de la maison.

Dieses Gebäude beherbergte früher öffentliche Toiletten und bestand aus einer Holzstruktur und vorgefertigten Paneelen. Die Lage war sehr günstig, aber die existierende Struktur befand sich in einem sehr schlechten Zustand. Das Betonfundament und einige Elemente der Holzstruktur wurden jedoch erhalten. Sie liegen jetzt unter einem neuen Dach, das das Haus Richtung Fluss öffnet. Das Dach besteht aus zwei nebeneinander liegenden und geneigten Ebenen, die über dem Gebäude schweben, wo sie von kleinen, runden Säulen festgehalten werden, die in den Wänden verankert sind. Die Vorderfront wurde durch einen Metallrahmen ersetzt, der einen Schirm aus doppeltem Glas hält, der verschoben werden kann. Die anderen Raumteiler wurden entfernt und die neue Aufteilung ging von den Wänden aus, die nicht bis zur Decke reichen. So ist das obere Fenster durchgehend und man nimmt den gesamten Raum des Hauses wahr.

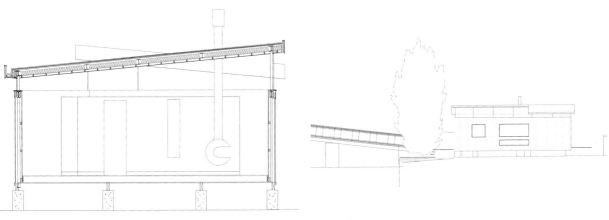

Cross section Section transversale Querschnitt     Elevation Élévation Aufriss

The iron chimney stands out as a sculptural element that dominates the interior of the house.

La cheminée en fer, suspendue à la couverture, devient, à l'intérieur de la maison, un élément de sculpture dominant.

Der Eisenkamin, der von der Decke hängt, wird zu einem skulpturellen Element, das den Raum beherrscht.

Different geometric objects and features mix to create a very rich space from a formal perspective.

Le jeu d'éléments et d'objets géométriques élémentaires crée un espace empreint d'une grande richesse formelle.

Durch das Spiel mit grundlegenden geometrischen Elementen und Objekten entstand ein Raum mit einem sehr großen Formenreichtum.

# ☐ Darmós House

## Maison Darmós

## Darmós Haus

Joan Pons Forment

Darmós is a small town in a rural Mediterranean setting surrounded by pine trees and vineyards. The project involved the refurbishment of an old house in the town; the result was a small independent residence on the top floor. One of the outstanding features of the renovation is the fact that one of the wings of the roof has not been rebuilt and the space has been used as a terrace, with views of the fields and the town. This has resulted in more space outdoors and an abundance of light indoors, entering through the terrace door and window. The small kitchen, with its views of the terrace and the exterior, is set practically in the center of the home, backing on to the eating area. The distribution of the spaces and furniture is modern in style, while the interior is imbued with a rustic atmosphere on account of the original stone walls and the simple decoration.

Darmós est une petite ville au coeur d'un paysage méditerranéen rural entourée de pins et de vignobles. Ce projet de restauration d'une vieille maison dans la ville a permis de réaliser une petite résidence indépendante au dernier étage. L'une des particularités particulièrement intéressante de cette rénovation, est de ne pas avoir reconstruit une des ailes du toit pour transformer l'espace obtenu en terrasse donnant sur les champs et la ville. Ceci a permis de gagner de l'espace extérieur et d'inonder l'intérieur de lumière naturelle, issue de la fenêtre et de la porte de la terrasse. La petite cuisine, avec vue sur la terrasse et l'extérieur, est installée au coeur de la maison s'adossant à la salle à manger. La distribution de l'espace et des meubles est d'inspiration moderne, l'intérieur étant imprégné d'une atmosphère rustique grâce aux murs d'origine en pierre et à la simplicité du décor.

Darmós ist eine kleine Stadt in einer ländlichen Umgebung am Mittelmeer, umgeben von Pinienwäldern und Weinbergen. Ein altes Stadthaus wurde modernisiert, so dass eine kleine, unabhängige Wohnung im obersten Geschoss entstand. Man verzichtete bei diesem Umbau bewusst darauf, einen der Dachflügel wieder aufzubauen, so dass eine Terrasse mit Blick auf die umgebenden Felder und die Stadt entstand. So schuf man mehr Platz im Freien und es fällt mehr Licht durch die Terrassentür und Fenster ins Innere. Von der kleinen Küche aus hat man einen Blick auf die Terrasse und auf die Umgebung. Sie liegt hinter dem Essbereich, praktisch im Zentrum der Wohnung. Der Raum und die Möbel sind auf moderne Art aufgeteilt. Die Atmosphäre wirkt durch die originalen Natursteine der Wände und die einfache Dekoration recht rustikal.

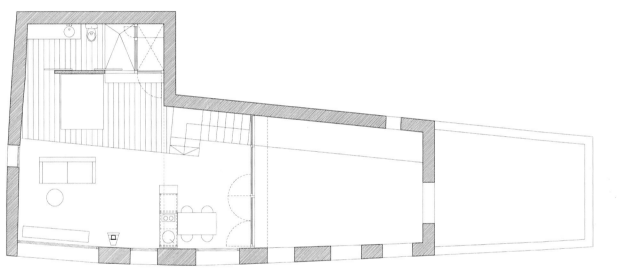

Plan Plan Grundriss

The layout has been calculated down to the last detail to make the most of the available space without sacrificing floor space or functionality.

La distribution du plan a été étudiée dans les moindres détails afin de maximaliser l'espace disponible sans sacrifier de surface au sol ou de fonctionnalité.

Die Wohnung wurde bis ins letzte Detail geplant, um den zur Verfügung stehenden Platz so gut wie möglich auszunutzen, ohne dabei an Raum oder Funktionalität zu verlieren.

As the considerable height allows the windows to be very large, the interior can receive abundant sunlight.

Les fenêtres, d'une hauteur considérable, sont très grandes, inondant ainsi l'espace intérieur de soleil.

Da die Wohnung relativ hoch ist, konnte man sehr große Fenster einbauen, so dass viel Sonnenlicht ins Innere fällt.

The small bathroom area, which backs onto a party wall, enjoys natural light and seems spacious.

La petite salle de bains, adossée à la cloison, bénéficie de lumière naturelle et semble spacieuse.

In das kleine Badezimmer, das hinter einer Wand liegt, fällt reichlich Tageslicht und es wirkt relativ groß.

# ☐ Loft in Gracia
## Loft à Gracia
## Loft in Gracia

Miquel Batlle, Michele Orliac

Different levels and platforms add depth and height to this small space, which is complemented with bright colors that emit bursts of energy. The entire apartment can be seen from the top floor, in the warm comfort of an elevated and discrete room, whose existence is insinuated behind a translucent curtain that allows those inside to see without being seen. The bedroom is placed as if it were in an attic, raised and yet always present, inviting itself into the other rooms. Nocturnal eyes have a panoramic view of the surroundings, recording scenes and movements that connect time to the broken planes of each object and inhabitant. The setting is empty in the center, the interior left open by pushing furniture and the other objects against the walls to permit totally free circulation.

Dans cet appartement, différents niveaux et plateformes confèrent profondeur et hauteur à un espace réduit, agrémenté de couleurs vives, vecteurs de dynamisme. Depuis l'étage supérieur, on a une vue d'ensemble sur l'appartement, lové au coeur d'une habitation chaleureuse, élancée et discrète, que l'on devine derrière un rideau translucide qui permet de voir sans être vu. La chambre à coucher, à l'image d'une mansarde, en hauteur et toujours présente, s'intègre délicatement au reste des pièces de la maison. La nuit offre une vision panoramique de l'habitation qui égrène son chapelet de scènes et de mouvements, au fil des heures, grâce à des plans fragmentés de chaque objet et habitant. La mise en scène dépouillée, laisse une entière liberté de circulation aux usagers, dans un intérieur qui confine les meubles et autres objets près des murs.

In dieser Wohnung setzte man verschiedene Ebenen und Plattformen dazu ein, Tiefe und Höhe innerhalb eines kleinen Raums zu schaffen. Diese Wirkung wird noch durch kräftige Farben verstärkt, die dem Raum viel Energie geben. Von der oberen Etage aus sieht man die ganze Wohnung. Dort liegt ein einladendes, sehr diskretes Zimmer, das durch eine lichtdurchlässige Gardine abgetrennt wird, so dass man sehen kann, ohne selbst gesehen zu werden. Das Schlafzimmer ist eine Mansarde, erhöht und doch immer anwesend, das sich den übrigen Räumen stets anbietet. Nachts hat man einen Panoramablick über die ganze Wohnung und betrachtet Szenen und Bewegungen der Objekte und Bewohner über die sich öffnenden Ebenen. Die Szenerie bleibt in der Mitte leer und ermöglicht eine völlige Bewegungsfreiheit für die Bewohner. Die Möbel und andere Objekte befinden sich an den Wänden.

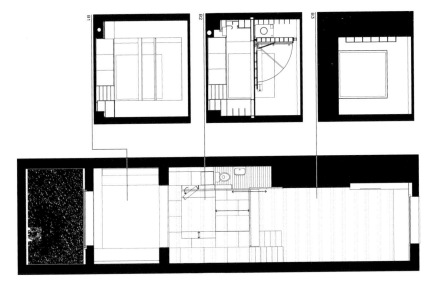

Plan Plan Grundriss

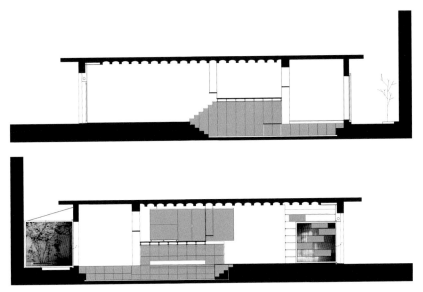

Sections Sections Schnitte

Depth and height are given to this small space through the use of different levels and platforms, set off by brilliant colours.

Différents niveaux et plateformes confèrent hauteur et profondeur à un espace réduit, agrémenté de couleurs vives.

Verschiedene Ebenen und Plattformen verleihen dem kleinen Raum Tiefe und Höhe. Sie werden noch durch kräftige Farben ergänzt.

The bedroom's sloping ceilings are noticeable from the other rooms in this home.

La chambre à coucher mansardée s'intègre délicatement au reste des pièces de la maison.

Das Schlafzimmer in der Mansarde deutet den übrigen Zimmern des Hauses seine Anwesenheit an.

The stage is empty, leaving occupants free to circulate through this interior, where furniture and other objects are placed close to the walls.

La mise en scène dépouillée, laisse une entière liberté de circulation aux usagers, dans un intérieur qui confine les meubles et autres objets près des murs.

Die Szenerie bleibt in der Mitte leer und ermöglicht eine völlige Bewegungsfreiheit für die Bewohner. Die Möbel und andere Objekte befinden sich an den Wänden.

# ☐ Optibo

White Group

The growing difficulties of construction and the cruel devastation of nature requires preventive architectural measures to define small inhabitable spaces. Optibo responds to this reality and presents a single multifunctional room that transforms itself according to the needs of the user from a central control panel. A limited setting contains in its apparent confinement all the scenarios of a conventional home. A scene-changing system powered by compressed air and electric and hydraulic energy causes the furnishings to appear and disappear through a 24-inch deep, hollow floor. The entrance key not only makes it possible for the occupant to access the interior of the house, it is also linked to the house when away, since it is able to control the alarm, and turn off the water and electricity. The chameleon-like illumination — consisting of fiber optics and LED lights — takes on the color appropriate to each situation.

La difficulté croissante de construction et la terrible dégradation de la nature exigent des mesures architecturales préventives pour définir de petits espaces habitables. Optibo répond à cette réalité et présente une habitation multifonctionnelle unique, modulable au gré des besoins de l'utilisateur depuis un panneau de contrôle central. Un scénario limité, contient dans son confinement apparent, toutes les mises en scène d'une habitation conventionnelle. Par le biais d'un système pneumatique de machinerie, alimenté à l'énergie hydraulique, les meubles apparaissent et disparaissent dans un renfoncement du sol de 60 cm de profondeur. La clé d'entrée permet à l'occupant d'accéder à l'intérieur de la maison et en même temps d'y être relié une fois parti, lui permettant ainsi de contrôler l'alarme, fermer l'eau ou éteindre la lumière. Un éclairage caméléon – doté de fibres optiques et de lumière LED – adopte la couleur appropriée à chaque situation.

Aufgrund der immer schwieriger werdenden Umstände für den Bau und der Verschlechterung der Umweltbedingungen wird es immer notwendiger, dass die Architektur kleine bewohnbare Räume schafft. Optibo hat als Antwort auf diese Anforderungen einen einzigen, multifunktionellen Raum geschaffen, der je nach den Ansprüchen und Notwendigkeiten des Benutzers über eine zentrale Steuerung verändert werden kann. In einem stark begrenzten Raum sind alle Szenarien einer konventionellen Wohnung enthalten. Durch ein pneumatisches System mit elektrischer und hydraulischer Energie verschwinden die Möbel, wie bei einem Bühnenwechsel, in einem 60 cm tiefen, hohlen Boden und tauchen wieder auf. Der Haustürschlüssel dient nicht nur zum Öffnen der Türe, sondern er ermöglicht dem Bewohner auch die Alarmanlage zu steuern sowie Wasser und Licht abzustellen. Eine sehr anpassungsfähige Beleuchtung aus Glasfaser und LEDs nimmt wie ein Chamäleon die für jede Situation geeignete Farbe an.

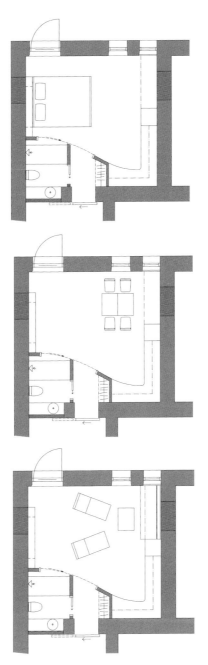

Plans Plans Grundrisse

Chameleon lighting – created with optical fibre and LEDs – takes on different colours under different circumstances.

Un éclairage caméléon – doté de fibres optiques et de lumière LED – adopte la couleur appropriée à chaque situation.

Die mit Glasfasern und LEDs geschaffene Beleuchtung nimmt wie ein Chamäleon je nach Situation eine andere Farbe an.

... pneumatic stage-machinery system, running on hydraulic energy, enables furniture to appear and disappear in a 60 cm cavity under the floor.

... le biais d'un système pneumatique de machinerie alimenté à l'énergie hydraulique, les meubles apparaissent et disparaissent dans un renfoncement du sol de 60 cm de profondeur.

... rch ein pneumatisches System mit elektrischer und hydraulischer Energie verschwinden die Möbel, wie bei einem Bühnenwechsel in einem 60 cm tiefen, hohlen Boden und tauchen ... eder auf.

A small stage the size of a bedroom contains backdrops to recreate every scene normally found in a conventional home.

Un scénario limité, comme la chambre à coucher, contient en apparence toutes les mises en scène d'une habitation conventionnelle.

Innerhalb eines begrenzten Raums wie dem Schlafzimmer sind alle Szenarien einer konventionellen Wohnung enthalten.

# Apartment in Madrid
## Appartement à Madrid
### Apartment in Madrid

Stone Designs

Inspired by the idea of turning a graphic image into a three-dimensional space and making it inhabitable, this house was configured by establishing strong visual links between the few different functional parts that compose it. This led to the idea of accentuating the contrast between the existing structure and the additions. The play of textures and colors created by the concrete and brick, and some intense brushstrokes of blue and pistachio green, establish planes that insinuate the necessary independence of the different spaces. Various icons related to the personality of the owner appear in different areas to define each one's assigned use. The green band that forms the dining room table and draws a continuous line in the kitchen, the living room, and the dining room, stands out from the rest of the elements.

Cette habitation, établissant de forts liens visuels entre les différents et rares espaces fonctionnels qui la composent, s'inspire de l'idée de transposition d'une image graphique dans l'espace tridimensionnel pour créer un lieu habitable. Dans ce contexte, il fallait exploiter le contraste entre la structure existante et les ajouts ultérieurs. Un jeu de textures et de couleurs, déterminé par le béton et la brique et quelques touches intenses d'azur et de vert pistache, établit des plans suggérant l'indépendance nécessaire des différents espaces. Divers icônes, reflétant la personnalité du propriétaire, apparaissent dans les diverses zones pour définir les fonctions. Une bordure verte – tracé délimitant la table de la salle à manger et qui se déroule en continue dans la cuisine, le séjour et la salle à manger – se détache des autres éléments.

Diese Wohnung schafft starke visuelle Verbindungen zwischen den verschiedenen und wenigen funktionellen Räumen, aus denen sie besteht. Die Planer waren von der Idee inspiriert, ein grafisches Bild auf einen dreidimensionalen Raum zu übertragen, so dass eine bewohnbare Umgebung entsteht. Diese Voraussetzung führte dazu, dass man den Kontrast der bereits existierenden Struktur und den späteren Anbauten ausnutzte. Ein Spiel aus Texturen und Farben, das von Beton, Ziegelstein und einigen intensiv blauen und pistaziengrünen Pinselstrichen bestimmt ist, dient dazu, die notwendige Unabhängigkeit der verschiedenen Bereiche anzudeuten. Diverse Ikonen, die mit der Persönlichkeit des Eigentümers zu tun haben, tauchen in verschiedenen Zonen auf, um die jeweilige Nutzung zu definieren. Ein grünes Band, das den Esszimmertisch formt und eine durchgehende Spur durch die Küche, das Wohnzimmer und das Esszimmer zieht, hebt sich von den übrigen Elementen ab.

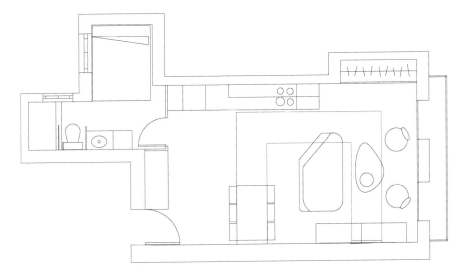

Plan Plan Grundriss

A green stripe, outlining the dining room table and crossing the kitchen, the living room and the dining room, stands out from the other elements.

Une bordure verte – tracé délimitant la table de la salle à manger et qui se déroule en continue dans la cuisine, le séjour et la salle à manger – se distingue des autres éléments.

Ein grünes Band, das den Esszimmertisch formt und eine durchgehende Spur durch die Küche, das Wohnzimmer und das Esszimmer zieht, hebt sich von den übrigen Elementen ab.

The play of textures and colors establishes different planes suggesting the independence of each individual space.

Un jeu de textures et de couleurs établit des plans qui suggèrent la définition des différents espaces.

Das Spiel mit Texturen und Farben schafft Ebenen, die die Unabhängigkeit der verschiedenen Bereiche andeuten.

# Loft in Milan
## Loft à Milan
## Loft in Mailand

Luca Mercatelli

This loft, located inside a building with access to the apartments from the exterior patio, had been the subject to previous modifications, but now its main challenge is functioning with the minimum possible amount of equipment required by a habitable unit. The design of the house focused on an attempt to combine the necessary comfort with the essence of natural and artificial light. The pragmatic solution was a modulable wall. The concept of horizontal planes and surfaces, determined by openings designed as pure, illuminated forms, gives rise to a living space for both day- and night-time use, a polygon adaptable to everyday needs. The surfaces slide to conceal and reveal elements when required, leaving the work of defining the space to memory, light, and function.

Placé à l'intérieur d'un édifice, avec un accès depuis le patio extérieur, ce loft, soumis précédemment à des modifications, est parfaitement bien équipé pour configurer une unité habitable. Le design de l'habitation qui essaie de conjuguer le confort nécessaire et l'essence – naturelle et artificielle – de la lumière, offre en réponse un mur équipé, solution pragmatique et modulable. La conception de plans horizontaux et de surfaces conditionnées par des ouvertures configurées comme des corps illuminés purs forme un espace habitable diurne et nocturne, qui se concrétise en un polygone inscrit, intégrant les activités quotidiennes. Les surfaces sont fluides, masquant ou dévoilant les éléments requis à un moment donné, laissant la mémoire, la lumière ou la fonction définir l'espace.

Dieses Loft im Inneren eines Gebäudes, zu dem man über den Hof gelangt, wurde schon vorher umgebaut und verfügt über die notwendigen Installationen, die es bewohnbar machen. Bei der Gestaltung der Wohnung konzentrierte man sich darauf, den notwendigen Komfort und die Essenz des Tageslichtes und des künstlichen Lichtes in Einklang zu bringen. Erstes Ergebnis ist eine Wand, die mit funktionellen, praktischen und flexiblen Elementen ansgestattet ist. Man arbeitete in waagerechten Ebenen und mit Oberflächen, die Öffnungen haben und als reine beleuchtete Körper gestaltet wurden, so dass ein Raum entstand, der tagsüber und nachts bewohnbar ist. Ein Vieleck, in dem die täglichen Aktivitäten stattfinden. Die Flächen werden verschoben, um die in jedem Moment notwendigen Elemente zu zeigen oder zu verbergen, so dass die Erinnerung, das Licht oder die Funktion den Raum definieren muss.

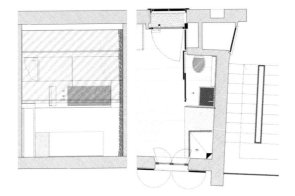

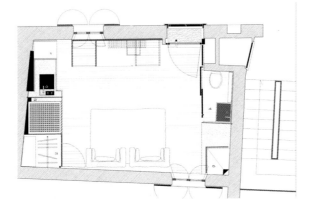

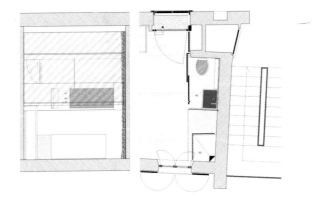

Plans Plans Grundrisse

This home has been designed to combine comfort with the presence of both natural and artificial light.

Le design de cette habitation tente d'allier confort et lumière artificielle ou naturelle.

Bei der Gestaltung dieser Wohnung versuchte man den Komfort mit dem Tageslicht und dem künstlichen Licht zu vereinen.

The furniture has been specially designed to meet the challenges posed by this small space: the couch, for instance, can be transformed into a bed.

Les meubles sont spécialement conçus pour répondre aux besoins d'un espace réduit : le divan, par exemple, est un lit convertible.

Die Möbel wurden speziell für diesen kleinen Raum entworfen. So kann zum Beispiel das Sofa in ein Bett verwandelt werden.

# ☐ All in One Piece
## Tout en un
## Alles in einem

Beriot, Bernardini & Gorini

This house is like a dollhouse that can be taken apart, and it is equipped with everything needed for carrying out household activities. The windows open to show new corners, the doors slide to form rooms and outline hallways, the stairway is sectioned so it will function as a closet: each object is a link and a possibility for transformation, diversification, spontaneity, and flexibility. A single box is visible, formed of multifunctional pieces that extend the interior, fulfilling a single function that starts the motor that activates daily life. An enormous closet opens to surprise us with the presence of a kitchen, sleeping like a ballerina in a music box that waits to be opened to welcome us at any moment. Inhabiting the ceiling or the intermediate space between this one and the floor, or accessing the most unexpected corner by a stairway, becomes reality.

Cette habitation, équipée de tous les ustensiles nécessaires à l'exécution des activités domestiques, est conçue comme une maison de poupées démontable. Les fenêtres s'ouvrent sous des angles nouveaux, les portes coulissantes façonnent les chambres et dessinent les couloirs, l'escalier se brise selon le profil d'une armoire : chaque objet est un trait d'union, un moyen de transformer l'espace, le moduler ou le diversifier spontanément et en souplesse. Une seule boîte composée de pièces polyvalentes pour élargir l'intérieur et accomplir une seule tache : mettre en marche le moteur qui active la vie quotidienne. Une armoire de grand format s'ouvre pour nous surprendre avec la cuisine, endormie, à l'instar de la danseuse d'une boîte à musique, abritée et toute prête à se mettre en mouvement pour nous éblouir, à tout moment. Habiter sous le toit, ou dans cet espace intermédiaire entre toiture et plancher, ou encore accéder par un escalier dans le coin le plus inattendu, devient réalité.

Diese Wohnung, die mit allem ausgestattet ist, was für die häuslichen Aktivitäten notwendig ist, wirkt wie ein Puppenhaus, das man wieder auseinander bauen kann. Die Fenster öffnen sich zu neuen Winkeln, die Schiebetüren formen Räume und zeichnen Flure, die Treppe wird unterbrochen, während sie der Form eines Schranks folgt. Jedes Objekt ist eine Verbindung und steht für Verwandlung, Aktion, Vielfalt, Spontaneität und Flexibilität. Eine einzige Kiste besteht aus multifunktionellen Teilen, die den Innenraum vergrößern, um eine einzige Funktion zu erfüllen: den Motor anzuwerfen, der das Alltagsleben startet. Ein großer Schrank öffnet sich und überrascht uns mit der Küche, die wie eine Tänzerin in einer Spieldose schläft und darauf wartet, herausgelassen zu werden, um uns jederzeit zu begrüßen. Das Dach oder diesen Raum zwischen dem Dach und dem Boden zu bewohnen oder über eine Treppe zu den unerwartetsten Winkeln zu gelangen, wird hier zur Realität.

In order to make the maximum use of the available space, a closet has been fitted under the removable stairs.

Pour optimiser l'espace disponible, une armoire a été installée sous l'escalier. Amovible, elle peut disparaître, si nécessaire.

Um den zur Verfügung stehenden Platz maximal auszunutzen, wurde ein Schrank unter der Treppe installiert. Außerdem ist sie mobil und man kann sie, falls notwendig, entfernen.

# ☐ White Apartment
## Appartement blanc
## Weißes Apartment

Marco Savorelli, Luca Mercatelli

There are still traces of the old apartment from the 1930s resting on the foundation of this house. The wooden beams across the ceiling show the imprint of time, with their scars and wrinkles. Their age combines with the youth of the more recent present to create a harmonious interior dominated by light, transparency, and fullness. Each of the elements that constitute the house occupies its own predetermined and permanent place, creating a balance that fills the interior with stability. The furniture set by the window opening on to the corridor form an ensemble of elements arranged in the only room designed to confront the puzzle of everyday life. An abstract composition with subtle touches, crossed by a small country path of stone and dry leaves that leads toward calm and stillness.

Cette habitation conserve les éléments de l'ancien appartement des années trente, sur lesquels repose cet édifice. Les poutres de bois qui traversent le toit reflètent les traces du temps passé, avec ses cicatrices et ses rides. Ancienneté et nouveauté du temps présent se côtoient, pour s'ouvrir sur un environnement tout en harmonie où prédominent, lumière, transparence et amplitude. Chacun des éléments, qui constituent l'habitation, a sa place attitrée, prédéterminée et permanente, créant un équilibre qui imprègne l'intérieur de stabilité. Les meubles installés près de la fenêtre s'ouvrant sur le corridor, sont une composition d'éléments mis en scène dans l'unique pièce qui absorbe les casse-tête de la vie quotidienne. Un cadre abstrait aux touches subtiles, traversé par un petit chemin champêtre de pierres et de feuilles sèches, qui nous conduit vers le calme et le recueillement.

In dieser Wohnung trifft man noch auf Spuren der alten Wohnung aus den Dreißigerjahren des letzten Jahrhunderts, in denen die Fundamente für dieses Gebäude entstanden. Die Holzbalken, die die Decke durchziehen, spiegeln den Lauf der Zeit wider, mit allen Narben und Falten. Ihr Alter lebt mit der Jugend der unmittelbaren Gegenwart zusammen, und sie verschmelzen zu einer harmonischen Umgebung, in der das Licht, die Transparenz und die Weite vorherrschen. Jedes der Elemente dieser Wohnung nimmt einen bestimmten und dauerhaften Platz ein. Der gesamte Raum wirkt stabil und ausgeglichen. Die Möbel lehnen sich aus dem Fenster, das zum Flur zeigt und stellen Fragmente eines einzigen Teils dar, das zum Puzzle des täglichen Lebens gehört. Ein abstraktes Bild mit winzigen Pinselstrichen, das von einem kleinen, ländlichen Weg aus Steinen und trockenen Blättern durchkreuzt wird, führt uns zur Ruhe und Geborgenheit.

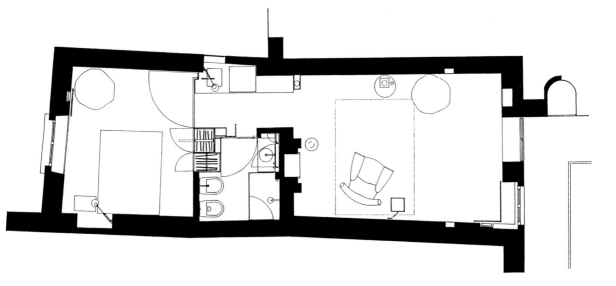

Plan Plan Grundriss

Contrasting materials and colors set up a dynamic effect in this small interior.

Le contraste entre les différents matériaux et les couleurs imprègne de dynamisme cet intérieur aux dimensions réduites.

Der Kontrast zwischen den verschiedenen Materialien und Farben verleiht diesem kleinen Raum sehr viel Dynamik.

e transparent glass walls enclosing the shower cubicle give the bathroom a sense of lightness and space.

s murs de verre transparent de la douche dotent la salle de bains de légèreté, accentuant la sensation d'amplitude.

e transparenten Glaswände der Dusche lassen das Bad sehr leicht und wesentlich größer wirken als es ist.

# ☐ Residence in Stockholm
# Résidence à Stockholm
# Wohnung in Stockholm

Claesson Koivisto Rune Arkitektkontor

Due to the apartment's small size, 763 sq. ft, the architects Claesson Koivisto Rune Arkitektkontor avoided the use of doors, except in the hall and bathroom. Though the partitions between the spaces run the entire height of the apartment, they do not quite touch the ceiling. This creates a relationship between rooms that enables the house to be perceived as a unit, like a collection of organic spaces. The communal areas, the living room, dining room, bathroom and kitchen, are located on the first floor. The partition wall that separates the dining room from the living room supports a staircase that leads to the upper level, where a small studio and a bedroom are located. As with most of their projects, these young architects used a small range of materials in the apartment: pale wood for the floors and furniture, a glazed mosaic in the bathroom and kitchen, a wool rug in the private areas and bright colors on some of the walls.

Etant donné la taille réduite de l'appartement, environ 70 m², le bureau d'architecture a éliminé les portes, à l'exception du vestibule et de la salle de bains. Presque toute la hauteur de l'appartement est parcourue de cloisons qui distribuent l'espace, sans parvenir, toutefois, jusqu'au plafond. Cela permet aux pièces d'être reliées entre elles et de percevoir l'habitation comme une unité. Les zones communes, le séjour, la salle à manger, la salle de bains et la cuisine sont au rez-de-chaussée. La cloison séparant la salle à manger du séjour sert de soutient à l'escalier conduisant au niveau supérieur qui accueille un petit studio et une chambre à coucher. Comme dans la plupart de leurs projets, les jeunes architectes ont utilisé un minimum de matériaux : bois clairs pour les sols et les meubles, mosaïque vitrifiée dans la salle de bains et la cuisine, un tapis de laine dans les zones privées et des couleurs vives sur certains murs.

Diese Wohnung ist nicht besonders groß, nur 70 m², deshalb vermied das Architekturstudio es, Türen einzubauen; nur die Diele und das Bad sind durch Türen abgetrennt. Fast die gesamte Höhe der Wohnung wird von Raumteilern eingenommen, die jedoch die Decke nicht berühren. So können die Räume miteinander verbunden werden und die Wohnung wird als eine Einheit empfunden. Die gemeinsamen Bereiche, also das Wohnzimmer, das Speisezimmer, das Bad und die Küche, liegen im ersten Stock. Die Trennwand, die das Speisezimmer vom Wohnzimmer absondert, dient als Halterung für die Treppen, die nach oben führen, wo ein kleines Atelier und ein Schlafzimmer liegen. Wie bei fast allen ihren anderen Raumgestaltungen benutzten die jungen Architekten nur sehr wenige Materialien: helles Holz für die Böden und Möbel, Mosaiken aus Glaskeramik in Bad und Küche, einen Wollteppich in den privateren Räumen und kräftige Farben an einigen Wänden.

This team of Swedish architects also specializes in industrial design, and has created furniture and other objects for their projects.

L'équipe d'architectes suédois, également spécialisée dans le design, a combiné meubles et objets de design à ses propres créations.

Das Team schwedischer Architekten ist auch auf Industriedesign spezialisiert, und so haben sie Designmöbel und Objekte mit eigenen Kreationen kombiniert.

The small kitchen is designed to meet every need without taking up any more space than is strictly necessary.

La petite cuisine est conçue pour répondre à toutes les fonctions requises sans pour autant occuper plus d'espace que nécessaire.

Die kleine Küche ist so gestaltet, dass sie allen Anforderungen genügt, ohne dass sie mehr Platz einnimmt, als eigentlich notwendig ist.

# □ 360 Loft

Schappacher White

This small space can become large enough to store a motorcycle inside without making it feel crowded. Large translucent fiberglass walls and sliding doors, as well as multiple built-in storage spaces, convey an airy feeling and expand the reduced dimensions of this attic, while disguising its limitations and raising doubts about its real dimensions. Magic tricks are performed and revealed all over the house behind curtains of illusion: an office is concealed behind the closet in the guest bedroom; stools become tables in the living room, and the water in the bathroom sink comes from the ceiling through stainless-steel pipes that the user controls with his or her feet. The kitchen hides many empty corners in the tall closet and in the long cabinet under the stone countertop.

Cet espace réduit peut s'élargir pour y garer une motocyclette à l'intérieur, sans étouffer l'atmosphère. Les grands murs, les portes coulissantes translucides de fibres de verre et les multiples espaces de rangement encastrés, oxygènent et amplifient les quelques mètres carrés qui constituent le grenier, tout en gomant ses limites et jetant un voile sur ses dimensions réelles. Toute la maison cache des procédés magiques derrière les rideaux de l'illusion : un bureau disparaît dans l'armoire de la chambre d'amis, les tabourets se métamorphosent en tables dans le séjour et le lave-mains de la salle de bains reçoit l'eau du toit grâce à des tubes d'acier inoxydable actionnés avec le pied. La cuisine cache de nombreux recoins vides, au sein de hautes armoires et dans le vaste espace de rangement, sous le plan de travail en pierre.

Dieser kleine Raum kann so groß werden, dass man sogar ein Moped darin parken könnte, ohne dass eine bedrückende Atmosphäre entsteht. Große lichtdurchlässige verschiebbare Wände und Schiebetüren aus Glasfaser und vielfach eingebauter Stauraum machen die wenigen Quadratmeter dieses Dachbodens sehr luftig und leicht und lassen ihn größer wirken. Außerdem verbergen sie seine Grenzen und erwecken Zweifel über die wahre Größe des Raums. Verborgene Tricks und Kniffe bestimmen das Design und veränden die Einrichtung wie von Geisterhand: Ein Büro versteckt sich im Schrank des Gästezimmers, die Hocker werden zu Tischen im Wohnzimmer, und das Handwaschbecken im Bad erhält Wasser von der Decke über Rohre aus Edelstahl, die der Benutzer mit den Füßen bedient. In der Küche sind zahlreiche leere Winkel in den hohen Schränken verborgen und der längliche Vorratsraum befindet sich unter der Arbeitsplatte aus Naturstein.

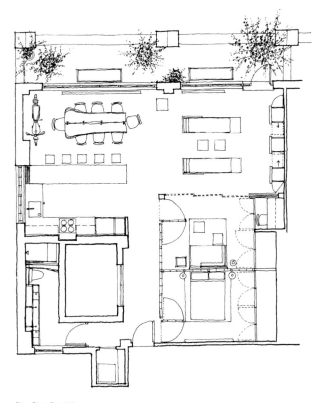

Plan Plan Grundriss

Translucent planes, outlined by optic-fiber doors and walls, organize and convert the rooms into an open, fluid space.

Des plans translucides, profilés par des portes et des murs en fibre optique, distribuent les pièces et les convertissent en un espace fluide et ouvert.

Lichtdurchlässige Ebenen, die von Türen und Wänden aus Glasfasern gerahmt sind, formen die Bereiche und werden zu einem durchgehenden, sehr offenen Raum.

The kitchen has plenty of empty space in the overhead units and the large storage cabinet under the stone worktop.

La cuisine recèle de nombreux coins vides dans les armoires hautes et dans la grande zone de rangement sous le plan de travail en pierre.

In der Küche sind zahlreiche leere Ecken in den hohen Schränken verborgen, und der längliche Vorratsraum befindet sich unter der Arbeitsplatte aus Naturstein.

## ☐ **Boston Apartment**
## **Appartement à Boston**
## Apartment in Boston

Messana O'Rorke Architects

The serious character of this apartment is lightened with splashes of informality and innovation. Despite its cold and conventional setting, there are refreshing corners where parties and activities alien to this domestic atmosphere can be improvised, all within a small space that refuses to be enclosed or suffer from an extremely limited configuration. The most intimate areas do not see any shame in undressing and are open to all viewers. Thus the bathroom can be seen from the kitchen, creating a sense that everything flows together naturally, without coercion. Some closets act as walls, a solution that emphasizes the connections and saves space. All the scenery in this small theater of custom and formality is open to view and suggests unlimited possibilities. Order and symmetry place each of the objects that make up the house in a precise, seemingly immutable position.

Empreint de sobriété, cet appartement décline une gamme de petits clins d'oeil informels et d'idées innovantes. Dans un environnement fait de signes conventionnels et froids, des coins plein de fraîcheur se détachent pour improviser des fêtes et des activités en dehors de l'univers domestique : tout cela dans un espace réduit, refusant d'être enfermé et cloisonné. Les zones les plus intimes n'éprouvent aucune pudeur à l'heure de se dénuder et s'ouvrent à tous les regards. En effet, la salle de bains est visible de la cuisine, conférant à l'ensemble de l'habitation une fluidité naturelle, sans contraintes. Certaines armoires servent de mur, solution réaffirmant les liens spatiaux et permettant un gain d'espace. Tous les décors de ce petit théâtre de formalités et habitudes sont visibles, offrant ainsi une myriade de possibilités. Grâce à l'ordre et à la symétrie, chaque objet constituant l'habitation, trouve sa juste place, presque immuable.

Dieses schlichte Apartment wird durch kleine, lustige Elemente und den Wunsch nach Erneuerung aufgeheitert. Obwohl die Umgebung konventionell und kalt ist, fühlt man, wie frei wirkender Raum entsteht, in dem man Feste und Aktivitäten improvisieren kann, die nichts mehr mit dem puren Wohnen zu tun haben, und das innerhalb eines kleinen Raums, der jedoch nicht eingeschlossen und begrenzt werden will. Die privateren Bereiche werden ohne Scham entblößt und den Blicken freigegeben. So kann man das Bad von der Küche aus sehen. Dadurch entstehen viele fließende Übergänge und keine Unterbrechungen. Einige der Schränke dienen als Wände, was die Räume ebenfalls miteinander verbindet und viel Platz spart. Die gesamte Dekoration dieses kleinen Theaters der Formen und Gebräuche ist sichtbar und bietet unendlich viele Möglichkeiten. Alle Objekte, die zu dieser Wohnung gehören, haben ihren genauen Platz. Außerdem sind sie beständig, was für Ordnung und Symmetrie sorgt.

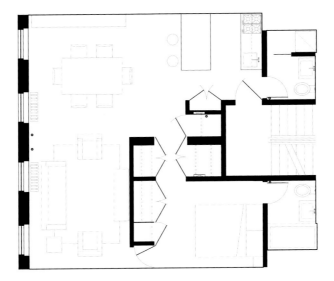

Plan Plan Grundriss

This small space is equipped with a variety of settings, all of which are on view and afford a wide range of possibilities.

Tous les décors de cet endroit de petites dimensions sont apparents et cachent une grande variété de possibilités.

Die gesamte Dekoration dieser kleinen Wohnung ist sichtbar und bietet eine Vielzahl von Möglichkeiten.

Order and symmetry govern every item in this house, endowing it with a marked sense of permanence.

Grâce à l'ordre et à la symétrie, chaque objet, intégrant l'habitation, trouve sa juste place, presque immuable.

Alle Objekte, die zu dieser Wohnung gehören, haben ihren genauen Platz. Außerdem sind sie beständig, so dass für Ordnung und Symmetrie gesorgt wird.

# ☐ House in the Coast
# Maison sur la côte
# Haus an der Küste

Joan Estrada

The aim of this project was to convert an old shop on the ground floor of a building into a residence for the interior designer who collaborated with the architects on this project. Since the space was set between party walls, the manipulation of natural light became the main feature of the design. It determined the form, the spatial distribution, and even the color of the project. The two existing façades were completely opened up with large windows that not only let light into the interior, but also linked it with the exterior. Sliding glass doors separating the centrally located bedrooms and bathroom allow light to enter and fully integrate these spaces with the rest of the house. White is the dominant color in all the areas, and only a few specific pieces of natural wood stand out in this continuous uniform setting.

L'objectif de ce projet est de transformer un ancien local situé au rez-de-chaussée d'une habitation pour la décoratrice intérieure elle-même, qui travaille sur le projet avec les architectes. Le local ayant des cloisons de séparation, l'exploitation de la lumière devient l'objectif premier de la conception. Les deux façades existantes ont été complètement ouvertes par le biais de grandes baies vitrées permettant à la fois le passage de la lumière et un lien constant avec l'extérieur. Les pièces centrales de l'habitation, les chambres à coucher et le cabinet de toilette, sont séparées par des portes coulissantes qui permettent l'entrée de la lumière et l'intégration totale au reste de l'habitation. Le blanc est la couleur qui domine dans toutes les pièces : seuls, quelques éléments en bois naturel, se détachent de ce cadre continue et uniforme défini par la façade immaculée et le carrelage en résine blanche.

Hier wurde ein ehemaliges Lokal im Erdgeschoss eines Gebäudes in eine Wohnung für den Innenarchitekten selbst umgebaut, wobei die Architekten an der Planung mitarbeiteten. In diesem Lokal gab es Trennwände, deshalb wurde es zum wichtigsten Ziel bei der Gestaltung, so viel Tageslicht wie möglich ins Innere zu leiten. Die beiden bereits vorhandenen Fassaden wurden durch weite Fenster vollständig geöffnet, so dass einerseits viel Licht in die Räume dringt und andererseits eine enge Verbindung zur Umgebung geschaffen wird. Die wichtigsten Räume der Wohnung, die Schlafzimmer und das Bad, sind ebenfalls durch verglaste Schiebetüren, durch die Licht fällt, abgetrennt. So werden auch diese Räume in die übrigen Bereiche der Wohnung integriert. Weiß ist die vorherrschende Farbe in allen Räumen. Es heben sich lediglich einige Elemente aus naturbelassenem Holz in diesem durchgehenden und einheitlichen Rahmen ab, der durch die weiße Fassade und den Boden aus weißem Kunstharz definiert wird.

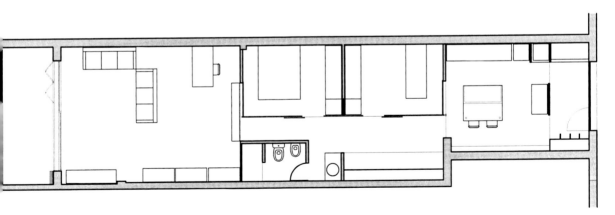

Plan Plan Grundriss

hanks to the layout and its white synthetic-resin flooring, this home is bright and open, with dynamic spatial communications.

irâce à la distribution et au carrelage en résine blanche, l'habitation est claire et ouverte, dotée d'espaces dynamiques.

ufgrund der Raumaufteilung und des Bodens aus weißem Kunstharz entstand eine klare und offene Wohnung, in die alle Räume dynamisch integriert sind.

# ☐ Dwelling in London
## Habitation à Londres
## Wohnung in London

AEM Architects

A lack of space often propels architects towards the most unpredictable transformations of the area available. Here, a mere 320 sq. ft of surface area, located on the attic floor of a nineteenth-century townhouse, was turned into a spacious and comfortable two-bedroom home. The height of the space was used to create an extra sleeping platform just under the ceiling, accessed by a steel-plate staircase which doubles as additional kitchen storage on the main floor. These innovative elements are complemented by simple modern furniture and fresh, pale light-reflecting colors — mainly white, contrasted with floating planes of orange, blue, and red, and the pale maple boards running along the floors. This wood is also used to clad the kitchen work surface, establishing visual coherence and spatial clarity throughout. Additional decoration is kept to a minimum, reducing the potential for visual clutter within the small area.

Très souvent, la pénurie d'espace conduit les architectes à réaliser les transformations les plus inattendues. Dans ce cas précis, les 30 m² situés à l'étage supérieur d'une maison individuelle du XIXè siècle, se sont convertis en une demeure spacieuse de deux chambres à coucher. Les architectes ont profité de la hauteur de l'espace pour créer une plateforme/chambre à coucher supplémentaire, à laquelle on accède par un escalier en plaques d'acier, servant également de rangement dans la cuisine. A ces éléments innovants et contemporains, s'ajoute un mobilier moderne aux couleurs claires qui reflètent la lumière : le blanc contraste avec les plans flottants de couleur orange, bleu et rouge, et les tons pâles de la structure à damier en bois d'érable, couvrent le sol. Le bois recouvre également le plan de travail de la cuisine, créant ainsi une unité visuelle et une clarté spatiale. La décoration, également réduite au minimum, diminue la possibilité de désordre visuel de l'espace.

Es kommt häufig vor, dass die Architekten die unglaublichsten Veränderungen vornehmen, weil es an Platz mangelt. In diesem Fall wurden 30 m² in einem Obergeschoss eines Einfamilienhauses aus dem 19. Jh. in eine großzügige Wohnung mit zwei Schlafzimmern verwandelt. Aufgrund der Höhe des Raumes konnte man eine zusätzliche Plattform für das Schlafzimmer schaffen, die man über eine Treppe aus Stahlblech erreicht, die gleichzeitig als Lagerraum für die Küche dient. Diese innovativen Elemente werden durch moderne und einfache Möbel und helle Farben ergänzt, die das Licht reflektieren. Die Farbe Weiß kontrastiert mit schwebenden Ebenen in orange, blau und rot, und mit den blassen Farben der strukturierten Ahorntafeln auf dem Boden. Auch die Arbeitsfläche der Küche ist aus Holz, wodurch der Raum visuell sehr einheitlich und klar wirkt. Es wurden sehr wenig Dekorationselemente eingesetzt, so dass keine visuelle Unordnung entsteht.

# ☐ Loft May

Lakonis Architekten

This interior, originally a six-room apartment in the center of Vienna, was converted into an open loft-style space for living and working. All the interior walls were demolished and the separation between the bathroom, kitchen, and bedroom was created with a single red wall. The idea was to create two zones, one near the interior patio, where the single-function rooms — the bathroom, kitchen, and bedroom — are located and another area facing the street, containing a large multifunctional room suitable for a range of activities. The changeable character of this space depends on who is using it and what activities are taking place in it. An effort was made to ensure that the materials and finishes of certain furnishings were related to the style of the original space.

Cet ancien appartement situé au centre de Vienne a été remodelé en un espace ouvert de type loft pour y vivre et y travailler. Toutes les cloisons sont éliminées, à l'exception d'un unique mur rouge qui sépare la salle de bains et la cuisine de la chambre à coucher. L'idée est d'obtenir deux zones différenciées : une première orientée vers le patio intérieur, où se trouvent les pièces unifonctionnelles, salle de bains, cuisine et chambre, et une deuxième zone orientée vers la rue, avec une grande pièce multifonctionnelle abritant diverses activités. La polyvalence de cet espace dépend de ses habitants et des activités qui s'y déroulent. Il fallait avant tout que les matériaux sélectionnés, tant pour les finitions que pour certaines pièces de mobilier, soient en harmonie avec le style original de l'espace.

Diese alte Wohnung im Zentrum von Wien wurde zu einem offenen Raum im Stil eines Lofts umgebaut, in dem man leben und arbeiten kann. Alle Trennwände wurden entfernt und das Bad, die Küche und das Schlafzimmer mit einer einzigen roten Wand abgetrennt. Es sollten unterschiedliche Zonen geschaffen werden, eine in der Nähe vom Innenhof, in der die Räume liegen, die nur einer Funktion dienen, nämlich das Bad, die Küche und das Schlafzimmer, und die andere zur Straße. In diesem zweiten Bereich liegt ein großer multifunktioneller Raum, in dem man verschiedenen Tätigkeiten nachgehen kann. Der wechselnde Charakter dieses Raums hängt von den Bewohnern und deren Aktivitäten in diesem Raum ab. Mit ausgewählten Materialien für die Gestaltung und bestimmten Möbeln wurde versucht, eine Beziehung zum einstigen Stil der Räume aufrecht zu erhalten.

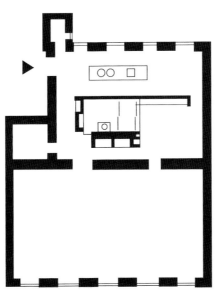

Plan Plan Grundriss

One of the aims was to select finishing and furniture materials fully compatible with the original style of these spaces.

Un des objectifs était de choisir des matériaux, tant pour les finitions que pour certains éléments du mobilier, qui soient en étroite relation avec le style original de l'espace.

Mit ausgewählten Materialien für die Gestaltung und bestimmten Möbeln wurde versucht, eine Beziehung zum einstigen Stil der Räume aufrechtzuerhalten.

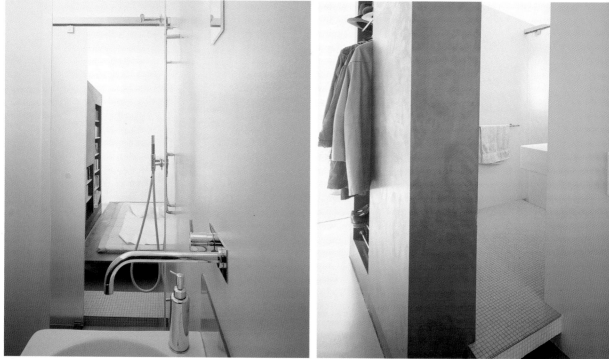

The bathroom floors are white mosaic, while linoleum has been fitted in the remainder of the apartment.

Le carrelage de la salle de bains est en mosaïques blanches, tandis que le reste des espaces de vie privée de l'habitation est recouvert de linoléum.

Das Badezimmer ist mit weißem Mosaik gefliest, während die übrigen Privaträume Linoleumböden haben.

# Drewes Apartment

## Appartement Drewes

## Drewes Apartment

Drewes & Strenge Architekten

This project is the result of the complete renovation of a conventional one-bedroom apartment. Some walls were eliminated, to create an open space and counteract the small size of the home, while others are secured with a double separation. The floor is partially raised and the ceiling is lowered in certain places. The furniture is designed and built around the perimeter of this architectural structure; it is personalized and completely integrated into the character of the apartment, forming a homogenous unit, an empty canvas where tranquility, sensual lighting and cool air currents can freely come into play. The uninterrupted space was designed without baseboards, door handles, light switches, and electrical outlets, as these would disrupt the smooth surface. Streaks of light accentuate specific objects, while at the same time forging the look of an evocative and comfortable environment.

Ce projet résulte de la rénovation intégrale d'un appartement conventionnel, avec une seule chambre à coucher. Afin d'obtenir un espace ouvert et généreux, dissimulant les dimensions réduites de l'habitation, certains murs ont été éliminés et d'autres consolidés par une double cloison. En outre, le carrelage a été partiellement relevé, et le toit surbaissé, par endroits. Le fil conducteur, tracé par les contours de cette structure architecturale, guide le design et la construction du mobilier, personnalisé et entièrement intégré à la nature de l'appartement. Une unité homogène, où le vide est roi, où le calme, les sinuosités de la lumière et l'air frais circulent librement. La trajectoire fluide de cette trame fait abstraction de portes, moulures, interrupteurs et de prises qui rideraient sa peau lisse. Des taches de lumière font ressortir des objets concrets, tout en façonnant l'esthétique d'une atmosphère suggestive et confortable.

Diese Wohnung entstand durch einen Gesamtumbau eines normalen Apartments mit einem Schlafzimmer. Man wollte einen offenen und weiten Raum schaffen und über die geringe Größe der Wohnung hinwegtäuschen. Dazu wurden einige Wände entfernt und andere in doppelter Entfernung befestigt. Auch der Boden wurde teilweise erhöht und die Decke in bestimmten Bereichen niedriger gemacht. Die Gestaltung und Konstruktion der Möbel folgt den Richtlinien dieser architektonischen Struktur. Alles in dieser Wohnung ist persönlich gestaltet und komplett integriert, so dass eine einheitliche Umgebung voller leerer Flächen entstand, wo die Ruhe, das Licht und die frische Luft sich frei ausbreiten können. Bei dieser ununterbrochenen Struktur verzichtete man auf Sockel, Türklinken, Gesims und Stecker, die die polierte Oberfläche erschüttern könnten. Lichtflecke unterstreichen konkrete Objekte, die gleichzeitig die Ästhetik einer anregenden und komfortablen Umgebung schaffen.

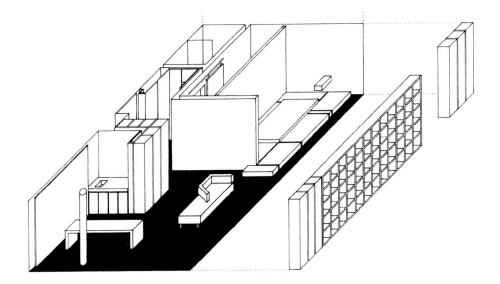

Perspective Perspective Perspektivzeichnung

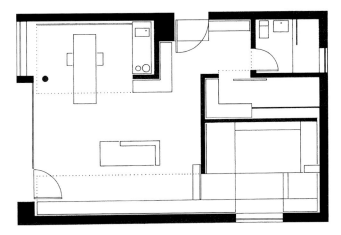

Plan Plan Grundriss

Shafts of light fall on various items, such as the pictures or the bookshelves, for functional purposes, while also intensifying the comfortable, evocative feel of this interior.

Divers faisceaux de lumière éclairent les objets, comme les cadres ou les étagères de livres, dans un but fonctionnel, tout en exaltant l'esthétique confortable qui émane de l'intérieur.

Verschiedene Arten Licht fallen auf Objekte wie Bilder oder Bücherregale. Sie erfüllen einen funktionellen Zweck, der gleichzeitig für Ästhetik und Komfort in den Räumen sorgt.

Each element fits into place in this abstract composition based on straight lines and regular planes.

Chaque élément s'intègre parfaitement à la composition abstraite de lignes droites et de plans réguliers qui forment l'habitation.

Jedes der Elemente passt perfekt in die abstrakte Komposition aus Geraden und rechteckigen Ebenen, die die Wohnung formen.

# Apartment in Barcelona
## Appartement à Barcelone
## Apartment in Barcelona

Located on the ground level of an urban building, this apartment establishes a strong link with its surroundings through the fragmented transparency of its large screened windows, allowing the maximum amount of contact with the exterior while at the same time providing the necessary security and protection. The restricted interior feels larger than it is, thanks to the small amount of furniture and objects, the bare essentials for a livable space within the high walls that mark the perimeter of the house. Foldout beds are hidden in the couches and the closet, which is in a single compact unit located next to the kitchen. This makes it easy to open up and vary the space as the beds do not create barriers that block access to the different areas. An atmosphere that verges on austerity creates a reclusive landscape, surrounding us with freedom, calm, and reflection in a place where we can connect with ourselves.

Situé au rez-de-chaussée d'un édifice urbain, cet appartement est fortement relié à l'environnement grâce à la transparence fragmentée de grandes baies vitrées grillagées optimalisant le contact avec l'extérieur tout en assurant la protection et la sécurité nécessaires. L'intérieur paraît plus grand grâce à un petit nombre de meubles et d'ustensiles, le strict nécessaire pour configurer un espace habitable sur le pourtour élevé des murs, délimitant les contours de l'habitation. Lits dépliables, escamotés dans le divan et dans l'armoire située juste à côté de la cuisine, facilitent l'organisation spatiale et la mobilité, évitant de barrer l'accès aux différentes zones, regroupées dans une même unité compacte et indissoluble. Une ambiance, frisant l'austérité, crée un paysage de retraite, nous enveloppant de liberté, calme et réflexion, pour nous retrouver nous-mêmes.

Dieses Apartment im Erdgeschoss eines städtischen Gebäudes stellt eine starke Verbindung mit seiner Umgebung her, und zwar durch die unterteilte Transparenz der großen, vergitterten Fenster, die für einen maximalen Kontakt mit der Außenwelt sorgen, gleichzeitig aber auch den notwendigen Schutz und Sicherheit bieten. Das Innere wirkt größer als es ist, weil nur wenig Möbel und Objekte vorhanden sind. Es gibt entlang den hohen Wänden, die die Wohnung einschließen, nur die Objekte, die für die Bewohnbarkeit des Raumes notwendig sind: Klappbetten, die in Sofas verborgen werden, ein Schrank direkt an der Küche, der als Raumteiler dient und für eine flexible Aufteilung sorgt. So wurden Barrieren vermieden, die den Zugang zu den verschiedenen Bereichen, die sich in dieser kompakten und untrennbaren Einheit befinden, verhindern würden. Die Atmosphäre ist sehr schlicht und es entstand eine Landschaft der Zurückgezogenheit, die den Bewohner mit Freiheit, Ruhe und Reflexion umgibt: ein Ort des Zusammentreffens mit uns selbst.

This austere, secluded environment creates a landscape of peace and quiet.

Une atmosphère, frisant l'austérité, crée un paysage de retraite qui nous calme et nous apaise.

Diese sehr schlichte Wohnumgebung schafft eine Rückzugsmöglichkeit, die Ruhe und Frieden vermittelt.

⌂ The folding beds are concealed within the couch and the closet, enhancing the spatial layout.

Les lits pliants, escamotés dans le divan et dans l'armoire, facilitent la distribution spatiale du lieu.

Die Klappbetten sind im Sofa und im Schrank verborgen, was die Aufteilung des Raumes vereinfacht.

# ☐ M&R House
## Maison M&R
### Haus M&R

Emmanuelle Marin, David Trottin

This house is set on a plot a mere 60 ft wide, surrounded by lush vegetation and with a gradient of 15%. Faced with these features, the architects opted to place the house along the length of the plot; it is spread over three different levels, with a few steps to help deal with the gradient. The public part is at the height of the entrance to the house, and as the land rises it leads to the bedrooms and the more intimate section of the house. As the house is tiered, it integrates into the terrain, and the views from both gardens mostly reveal only the narrow sides, allowing the house itself to go almost unnoticed. A relationship between the exterior and the interior was created at both ends of the house, by means of large windows that serve to both reinforce the feeling of spaciousness and turn these spaces into rooms belonging to the house.

Cette maison se trouve sur un terrain ne faisant que 18 m de large, avec une pente de 15% et entouré d'une végétation exubérante. Vu les caractéristiques du terrain, les architectes ont choisi de situer la maison dans le sens de la longueur et de l'articuler autour de trois niveaux, avec des marches pour accéder à chacun d'entre eux. La zone publique est à la hauteur de l'entrée de la maison : à mesure qu'il s'élève, le terrain mène aux chambres à coucher et aux zones plus intimes de la maison. La maison, ainsi échelonnée, épouse le terrain. Les vues depuis les deux jardins ne révèlent que les côtés étroits, cachant presque l'édifice. En outre, la relation entre l'intérieur et l'extérieur est très forte aux deux extrémités de la maison, grâce à de grandes fenêtres qui soulignent la sensation d'amplitude, convertissant ces espaces en pièces qui font partie intégrante de la maison.

Dieses Haus befindet sich auf einem Grundstück, dass nur 18 m breit ist, eine Neigung von 15% hat und von einer üppigen Vegetation umgeben ist. Aufgrund dieser Eigenschaften entschieden sich die Architekten dafür, das Haus in Längsrichtung zu bauen und auf drei Ebenen anzulegen, die über Stufen miteinander verbunden sind. Der gemeinsam genutzte Bereich befindet sich am Eingang zum Haus. Während man den Erhöhungen des Hauses, die vom Gelände vorgegeben sind, folgt, erreicht man die Schlafzimmer und privateren Wohnbereiche. Durch diese Stufenform fügt sich das Haus in das Gelände ein und von beiden Gärten aus sieht man nur den schmalen Teil des Hauses, so dass es fast verborgen bleibt. Außerdem entstand zwischen den beiden Enden des Hauses durch große Fenster eine starke Beziehung zwischen innen und außen. Der Raum wirkt weit und die Umgebung wird zu einem Bestandteil des Hauses.

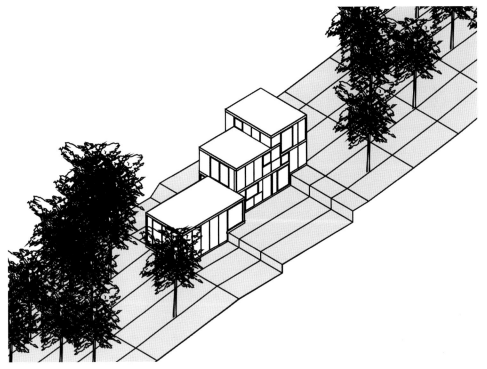

Axometry Axonométrie Axonometrische Ansicht

Thanks to their small dimension and transparency, the narrower façades pass unnoticed from the garden.

De petite taille et transparentes, les façades les plus étroites de la maison passent presque inaperçues depuis les jardins.

Aufgrund der geringen Größe und der Transparenz nimmt man die schmalen Fassaden des Hauses vom Garten aus fast nicht wahr.

# House in Kromeriz
# Maison à Kromeriz
# Haus in Kromeriz

Archteam

The architects responsible for this project, located in a semi-rural garden in the city of Kromeriz, describe it as a suite in the middle of a garden. Its limited – barely 800 sq. ft – make it into a compact structure closed at each end but open toward the garden via the porch and windows. The open-plan interior is spread over two floors, with a gallery on the top floor. The house is made of wood, although the surfaces are covered with membranes that act as thermal insulation and waterproofing for the interior. Titanium and zinc panels were fitted on the roof. A staircase with projecting steps leads to the upper level, with its private rooms and gallery. The house gains extra space as a result of the outside porch, with a strip of wood attached to the main structural framework. This area can be put to use when the temperature allows.

Les architectes qui ont conçu cette maison, située dans un jardin semi rural de la ville de Kromeriz, la définissent comme un élément de mobilier au cœur d'un jardin. Ses dimensions réduites, à peine 75 m², en font une structure compacte qui se referme en longueur sur son axe et s'ouvre vers le jardin par le biais de ses baies vitrées et du porche. L'intérieur, ouvert, s'articule sur deux niveaux avec une galerie à l'étage supérieur. La maison est en bois, avec des surfaces recouvertes de membranes agissant en isolant thermique, tout en imperméabilisant l'intérieur. Des plaques de titane et de zinc sont implantées dans la toiture. Un escalier aux marches en saillie conduit au niveau supérieur, accueillant les pièces privées et la galerie. L'habitation gagne de l'espace grâce au porche extérieur, constitué d'une planche de bois tendue sur la structure principale. C'est un espace additionnel utilisable en fonction de la température.

Die Architekten, die dieses Haus in einer Parkanlage in der Stadt Kromeriz planten, definieren es als ein Möbelstück mitten in einem Garten. Das Haus ist mit seinen 75 m² sehr klein. Es ist als eine kompakte Struktur konstruiert, die sich längs über eine Achse schließt und zum Garten hin über die Fenster und die Veranda öffnet. Das Innere ist offen, es gibt zwei Etagen und eine Galerie im Obergeschoss. Das Haus ist aus Holz, obwohl die Oberflächen mit Membranen verkleidet sind, die als Wärme- und Kälteisolierung und Schutz vor Feuchtigkeit dienen. Auf dem Dach wurden Platten aus Titan und Zink installiert. Eine Treppe mit frei schwebenden Stufen führt nach oben, wo sich die privateren Räume und die Galerie befinden. Durch die Terrasse vor dem Haus wird Platz gewonnen. Sie besteht aus einer Holzplatte, die an der Hauptstruktur befestigt ist. So wurde ein zusätzlicher Raum geschaffen, der genutzt werden kann, wenn das Wetter schön ist.

Plans Plans Grundrisse

The open-plan interior is spread over two floors, with a gallery on the top floor. An distinctive staircase with projecting steps leads to the upper level.

La maison s'articule sur deux étages avec une galerie additionnelle dans la partie supérieure, à laquelle on accède par le biais d'un escalier original, doté de marches en saillie.

Das Haus erstreckt sich über zwei Etagen und eine zusätzliche Galerie in der oberen Etage, die man über eine originelle Treppe mit frei schwebenden Stufen erreicht.

The house gains extra space as a result of outside porch, built from a strip of wood attached to the main structural framework.

L'habitation gagne de l'espace grâce au porche extérieur, fabriqué d'une planche de bois tendue sur la structure principale de la maison.

Durch die Terrasse vor dem Haus wird Platz gewonnen. Sie besteht aus einer Holzplatte, die an der Hauptstruktur befestigt ist.

# ☐ Boathouse
## Maison bateau
## Bootshaus

Drew Heath

One of the aims of this project was to redesign the concept of the boathouse, or, looking at it from a different perspective, boats designed as houses floating on the water. The typical Australian model is based on a box-like structure that floats on pontoons. The project began with the installation of a covered railing on the deck around the boat that opens up the interior to the views of the ocean. This became a small pavilion that floats on the water. The dining room and the kitchen were placed in the front of the boat, while the main bedroom, a smaller bedroom, and the bathroom were located at the other end. The walls and the beams were constructed with a lightweight wood, and the roof structure was covered with metal. Boathouse is a very small building compared to a house in the city or in the country, since it only measures about 380 sq. ft. It therefore adopts measures to compress space, such as functional storage units and a reduced kitchen area.

Un des objectifs de ce projet était de revisiter le concept de la maison bateau c'est-à-dire de bateaux aménagés en maisons flottantes sur l'eau. Le modèle australien type est basé sur une structure en forme de boîte qui dépasse des pontons. Les opérations d'aménagement ont débuté par l'installation d'une rambarde avec une toiture débordant autour du bateau pour ouvrir l'intérieur et profiter des vues sur la mer : il en résulte un petit pavillon flottant. La salle à manger et la cuisine sont regroupées sur l'avant du bateau, l'extrémité opposée accueillant la chambre à coucher, une petite pièce et la salle de bains. Les murs et les poutres sont en bois léger, tandis que la structure du toit a été recouverte de métal. Comparée à une maison en ville ou à la campagne, c'est une très petite habitation d'environ 30 m² : rangements fonctionnels et réduction de l'espace cuisine, par exemple, sont les solutions pour comprimer l'espace.

Eines der Planungsziele war es, das Konzept des Bootshauses neu zu gestalten, also ein Haus auf dem Wasser zu schaffen. Das typische australische Modell basiert auf einer kistenförmigen Struktur, die aus der Schiffsbrücke ragt. Der Eingriff begann, als man ein Geländer mit einer Abdeckung um das Boot errichtete, um das Innere zu öffnen und den Blick aufs Meer freizugeben. So entstand ein kleiner, schwimmender Pavillon. Das Esszimmer und die Küche befinden sich vorne im Boot, und auf der anderen Seite liegen das Schlafzimmer, ein weiteres kleines Zimmer und das Bad. Die Wände und die Balken sind aus leichtem Holz. Die Dachstruktur wurde mit Metall verkleidet. Im Vergleich zu einem Haus in der Stadt oder auf dem Land ist diese Wohnung sehr klein, die Nutzfläche beträgt ungefähr 30 m². Deshalb wurden funktionelle Lagermöglichkeiten geschaffen und Räume wie die Küche sehr klein gehalten.

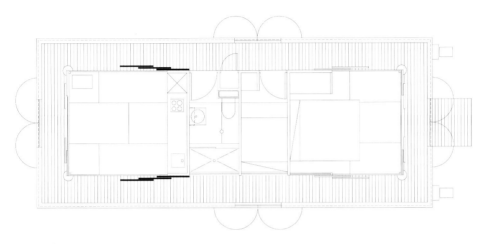

Plan Plan Grundriss

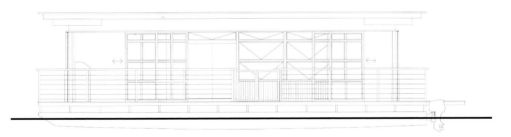

Section Section Schnitt

The rooms open to the exterior, making maximum use of natural daylight and the magnificent sea views.

Les chambres s'ouvrent sur l'extérieur, bénéficiant de la lumière naturelle et de splendides vues sur la mer.

Die Zimmer öffnen sich nach außen und lassen viel Tageslicht hinein. Man hat einen wundervollen Blick aufs Meer.

To make up for the lack of space, storage solutions such as the compact design for the kitchen have been devised.

Pour remédier au manque d'espace, on a envisagé des solutions de rangement fonctionnel, à l'instar de la cuisine, de forme très compacte.

Um den Platzmangel auszugleichen, wurden funktionelle Stauräume geschaffen und die Küche wurde sehr klein gehalten.

## Steely Residence
## Résidence Steely
## Haus Steely

Craig Steely

This house, situated 20 miles from the Kilauea volcano in Hawaii, is set on the only remaining black sand beach on this part of the island. During the day, a column of smoke is visible where the lava meets the ocean; by night the glow of the volcano is reflected in the clouds. A projecting platform floats 7 ft above the lava, to minimize the environmental impact. The natural setting called for ecologically-friendly solutions: one of these is the use of water collected from the roof and stored in a concrete cistern, before being recycled in the garden. Furthermore, the house adapts itself to atmospheric conditions by means of curtains, screens and blinds, which control the lighting and the ventilation.

Cette maison, située à 32 km du volcan Kilauea, à Hawaï, est implantée sur l'unique plage de sable noir qui reste de ce côté de l'île. Le jour, on peut observer une colonne de fumée qui se forme là où la lave s'unit à l'océan. De nuit, les feux du volcan se reflètent dans les nuages. Une plateforme en saillie flotte deux mètres au-dessus de la plage de lave, réduisant ainsi au minimum l'impact sur le paysage. Pour cette habitation, l'environnement naturel oblige d'envisager des alternatives écologiques, l'une d'elles étant l'utilisation de l'eau employée dans le jardin : recueillie dans la toiture en forme d'aile de mouette, elle est emmagasinée dans la citerne de béton. De surcroît, la maison s'adapte aux conditions atmosphériques grâce aux rideaux, cloisons et persiennes, contrôlant la lumière et la ventilation.

Dieses Haus, 32 km von dem Vulkan Kilauea auf Hawaii entfernt, steht auf dem einzigen Strand mit schwarzem Sand, den es in dieser Gegend der Insel gibt. Am Tag sieht man eine Rauchsäule dort aufsteigen, wo die Lava in den Ozean fließt. Nachts spiegelt sich der Glanz des Vulkans in den Wolken wider. Eine Plattform schwebt zwei Meter frei über der Lava, damit die Landschaft so wenig wie möglich verändert wird. Die Umgebung machte es notwendig, ökologische Lösungen für dieses Haus zu finden. Eine davon ist das Wasser, das in Haus und Garten verbraucht wird, durch das Dach in Form eines Möwenflügels aufgefangen und in einer Betonzisterne gespeichert wird. Außerdem wird das Haus mithilfe von Gardinen, Schirmen und Jalousien an die Wetterbedingungen angepasst. So wird das Sonnenlicht und die Luftzufuhr kontrolliert.

The interior is finished entirely in wood, which provides a warm and homely feel.

L'intérieur de la maison est entièrement revêtu de bois, une matière qui octroie chaleur et confort.

Im Inneren ist das Haus vollständig mit Holz verkleidet, wodurch eine warme und gemütliche Atmosphäre entsteht.

The house adapts itself to atmospheric conditions by means of curtains, screens and blinds, which control the lighting and the ventilation.

L'habitation s'adapte aux conditions atmosphériques grâce aux rideaux, cloisons et persiennes qui contrôlent la lumière et la circulation de l'air.

Außerdem wird das Haus mithilfe von Gardinen, Schirmen und Jalousien an die Wetterbedingungen angepasst. So werden das Sonnenlicht und die Luftzufuhr kontrolliert.

# ☐ Keenan Tower
## Tour Keenan
### Keenan Turm

Marlon Blackwell

This project allows the owner to continue living the dream that most people relinquish when they reach adulthood. This high tower, which can only be accessed using a metal spiral staircase, contains a refuge measuring 560 sq. ft. Close observation reveals a project that can be defined either as functional or aesthetic, depending on the viewpoint. A staircase connects the base of the tower to the hall, where the light and the views disappear momentarily, only to reappear again at the top, where the residence itself is located. Here, a single room holds the living and sleeping areas, surrounded by a running window that floods the space with natural light. Folding stairs lead to the top level, which contains an exterior patio with openings that direct the gaze upwards toward the tree-top canopy. The stairs are located inside a structure of vertical wood boards.

Ce projet a permis au propriétaire de réaliser un rêve que beaucoup abandonnent à l'âge adulte. Les hauteurs d'une tour, à laquelle on accède par un escalier en colimaçon métallique, abritent un refuge de 52 m². Vu de plus près, ce projet affiche une perspective fonctionnelle et esthétique : l'escalier enlace le pied de la tour avec le vestibule, où lumière et vues s'effacent un instant pour réapparaître dans la partie supérieure où se love l'habitation. Une pièce unique abrite le séjour et la chambre à coucher, flanquée d'une fenêtre coulissante qui inonde l'espace de lumière. Un escalier escamotable conduit au niveau supérieur, un patio aux ouvertures dirigées vers le toit arboré. L'escalier, à l'image d'un tronc creux, se situe à l'intérieur d'un treillis de lattes de bois verticales.

Mit diesem Haus hat sich der Kunde einen Kindertraum erfüllt, auf den die meisten von uns verzichten, wenn sie einmal erwachsen geworden sind. Oben auf dem Turm, den man über eine Wendeltreppe aus Metall erreicht, befindet sich ein 52 m² großer Zufluchtsort. Wenn man sich diese Wohnung genauer betrachtet, bemerkt man, wie funktionell und gleichzeitig ästhetisch sie ist. Die Treppe verbindet die Basis des Turms mit der Diele, wo das Licht und der Ausblick einen Moment verloren gehen, um gleich darauf im oberen Teil, wo sich die Wohnung befindet, wieder aufzutauchen. Dort sind in einem einzigen Raum das Wohnzimmer und das Schlafzimmer untergebracht. An der Seite befindet sich ein Fenster, durch das der Raum mit Licht durchflutet wird. Eine klappbare Treppe führt nach oben, zu einem Hof mit Öffnungen, durch die man auf eine Decke aus Bäumen schaut. Die Treppe, die einem hohlen Stamm gleicht, befindet sich im Inneren eines Flechtwerks aus vertikalen Holzleisten.

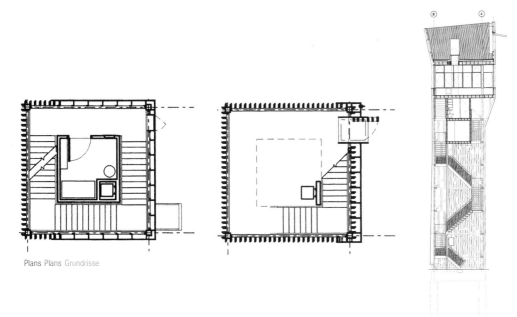

Plans Plans Grundrisse

Section Section Schnitt

...rganic materials (oak timber) for the exterior structure contrast with the white steel panels on some of the façades.

...e matériau organique (bois de chêne) de la structure extérieure, contraste avec les panneaux blancs en acier qui revêtent une partie des façades.

...as organische Material (Eichenholz) der äußeren Struktur steht im Gegensatz zu den weißen Stahlpaneelen, mit denen ein Teil der Fassade verkleidet ist.

The use of light materials like steel and wood allow light to penetrate from both sides.

L'emploi de matériaux légers, comme l'acier et le bois, permet à la lumière de pénétrer l'intérieur des deux côtés.

Die Verwendung leichter Materialien wie Stahl und Holz lässt das Licht von beiden Seiten in das Innere strömen.

# Armadillo House
# Maison tatou
## Gürteltierhaus

24H Architecture

Situated on the shore of Lake Övre Gla, in the Glasgoken nature reserve, this house was built as an extension to a pre-existing cabin by imitating the natural environment in which wood is the main building element. The new house is easily adaptable to weather conditions, seasonal variations and changes in the number of occupants by means of an extendible structure, which provides a double layer during the winter, a protected terrace during the summer and an inner space to accommodate guests. One of the main construction aims was to take full advantage of the magnificent views of the surrounding countryside. On one side, the glass windows open towards the woods, whilst on the other side, the elevated position of the house provides superb vistas across the lake.

Construite en prolongement d'une cabane préexistante, datant du XIXe siècle, cette maison située au bord du lac Övre Gla, dans la réserve naturelle de Glasgoken, imite la nature qui l'entoure par le biais d'une ossature construite essentiellement en bois. La nouvelle habitation s'adapte librement aux conditions atmosphériques, aux saisons ou au nombre d'occupants, grâce à une structure extensible qui crée une double enveloppe durant l'hiver, une terrasse protégée en été et un espace intérieur pour loger les hôtes. Un des objectifs fondamentaux de la construction est de profiter des vues magnifiques sur le paysage environnant. D'un côté, les baies vitrées s'ouvrent vers le bois et, de l'autre, la situation en hauteur de la maison privilégie la contemplation des magnifiques vues sur le lac.

Dieses Ferienhaus am Ufer des Sees Övre Gla in einem Naturpark in Glasgoken wurde als Erweiterung einer bereits existierenden Hütte aus dem 19. Jh. errichtet. Es imitiert in seiner, vor allem aus Holz bestehenden Struktur, die Natur, von der es umgeben ist. Das neue Haus kann beliebig an das Wetter, die Jahreszeit oder die Anzahl der Bewohner angepasst werden. Dazu dient eine ausziehbare Struktur, die während des Winters eine kompakte, zweite Haut bildet und im Sommer eine geschützte Terrasse ist, sowie einen weiteren Raum, der als Gästezimmer dient. Eines der wichtigsten Ziele beim Bau dieses Hauses war, dass man aus den Räumen einen Blick auf die schöne Landschaft der Umgebung haben sollte. Auf der einen Seite blickt man durch die Fenster auf den Wald, auf der anderen Seite hat man durch die erhöhte Lage einen wundervollen Blick auf den See.

...uring the winter, the double-thickness structure provides insulation and confers a warm and natural feel.

...n hiver, la structure doublée sert d'isolant thermique tout en transmettant une sensation à la fois chaleureuse et naturelle.

...m Winter dient die doppelt verstärkte Struktur als Isolierung und lässt das Haus warm und natürlich wirken.

During the summer, the terrace becomes an additional interior space.

En été, la terrasse se transforme en un espace intérieur d'appoint.

Im Sommer wird die Terrasse zu einem zusätzlichen Wohnraum.

# Cocoon House
## Maison Cocoon
### Cocoon Haus

Michael Bellemo, Cat MacLeod

This unique house, designed by architects Cat MacLeod and Michael Bellemo, is located amidst the thick forest of the Wye River area. The structure, which can be seen from all angles because of the steepness of the hills, stands out against the surrounding vegetation. The steel covering creates a texture that mimics an animal's outer shell, in an attempt to integrate the volume into the environment. The Cocoon House results from the consolidation of opposing concepts, including the formal interest of a rectangular shape within a curved volume, inanimate elements against organic ones, and smoothness against roughness. The design had to promote an open approach towards the landscape and at the same time provide a sturdy shelter against the area's normally harsh weather. The result is this perfectly symmetrical volume that resembles a zeppelin, and was constructed using aeronautical technology. It is a magnificent example of the fusion of pragmatism and poetry.

Au coeur de la dense forêt qui forme le paysage de la zone de Wye River, se love cette résidence originale. Grâce à la forte pente du coteau, l'habitation peut être admirée de tous les côtés et sa structure extérieure métallique se détache de la végétation environnante. La maison Cocoon est régie par la rencontre de contrastes, concrétisée par le concept formel du rectangle à l'intérieur d'un volume incurvé, l'inanimé face à l'organique et la douceur face à la rigueur. Le design devait favoriser l'ouverture vers le paysage et construire simultanément un refuge face aux intempéries fréquentes. Il en résulte un volume parfaitement symétrique en forme de zeppelin, construit à partir de technologies relevant du secteur aéronautique. Un magnifique exemple de fusion entre pragmatisme et poésie.

Mitten in einem dichten Wald in der Region des Wye River liegt dieses einzigartige Haus, das von den Architekten Cat MacLeod und Michael Bellemo geplant wurde. Aufgrund der starken Neigung des Hügels kann man das Haus von allen Seiten gut sehen. Seine Metallstruktur hebt sich von der umgebenden Vegetation ab. Die Gestaltung dieses Hauses beruht auf dem Prinzip des Zusammenspiels von Gegensätzen: eine rechteckige Form in einer gekrümmten Masse, das Leblose im Gegensatz zu dem Organischen, und die Weichheit, die sich der Härte gegenüberstellt. Das Haus sollte sich zur Landschaft hin öffnen und gleichzeitig ein Zufluchtsort sein, in den man sich bei dem rauhen Wetter in dieser Region zurückziehen kann. So entstand eine perfekt symmetrische Zeppelinform, die mit der Luftfahrt entlehnten Techniken konstruiert wurde. Ein wundervolles Beispiel dafür, wie man den Pragmatismus mit der Poesie in Einklang bringen kann.

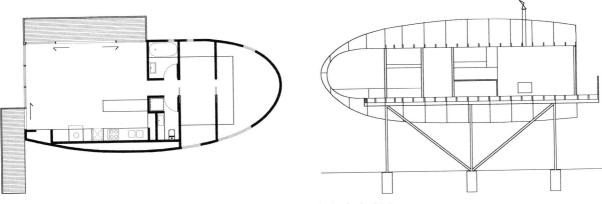

Plan Plan Grundriss             Section Section Schnitt

The rectangular wooden façade with a glass front is the sole interruption in this uniform, airtight outer shell.

Le rectangle de bois de la façade de verre est l'unique élément qui brise l'uniformité hermétique de la toiture.

Das Holzrechteck an der verglasten Fassade ist die einzige Unterbrechung der hermetischen Einheitlichkeit des Panzers.

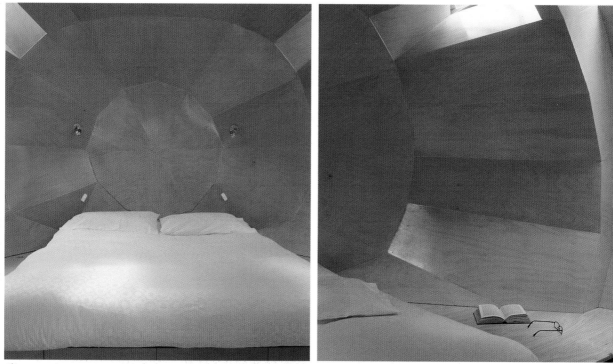

In contrast with the sitting room's rectangular ceiling, the two bedroom "booths" take on the oval shape of the outer shell.

En opposition au plafond rectangulaire du salon, les murs des deux cabines/chambres à coucher définissent la forme ovale de l'enveloppe extérieure.

Im Gegensatz zu dem rechteckigen Dach des Wohnzimmers haben die Wände der beiden Schlafkabinen die ovale Form der äußeren Schicht.

## ☐ Markies Caravan
## Roulotte Markies
## Wohnwagen Markies

Eduard Böhtlingk

The Dutch word for awning, markies, is the name given to this camper, which contains a hidden space within its conventional shape, ready to be quickly and easily opened at any moment if the need arises, to enlarge the small dimensions of the main structure. Two wings mysteriously appear to transform the rectangular shape of the nomadic house into an open fan, which looks like the magic feathers of a peacock in an attractive and ostentatious pose. Three areas intended as backdrops to the different acts of the daily drama can be seen in the basic camper. A middle part, consisting of the permanent immobile core of the dwelling, fulfills the functions of kitchen, dining room, and bathroom. The two temporary areas turn into a terrace when the weather permits.

Le mot hollandais pour vélum, « markies », est le nom d'une roulotte contenant, au sein de ses dimensions conventionnelles, un espace caché prêt à être installé à tout moment, très vite et facilement, pour rallonger les dimensions réduites de la structure principale. Comme par enchantement, deux ailes apparaissent pour modifier la silhouette rectangulaire de la maison nomade en un éventail ouvert, qui s'exhibe à l'instar des plumes magiques du paon, en un geste attirant et ostentatoire. Trois zones destinées à mettre en scène les différents actes de la vie quotidienne, peuvent être tirées de l'essence même de la roulotte. Une partie centrale, représentée par le tronc fixe et permanent de l'habitation, fait office de cuisine, salle à manger et salle de bains. Les deux zones temporaires se transforment en terrasses, quand il fait beau.

Das holländische Wort für Markise, „markies", ist der Name eines Wohnwagens, in dem sich, innerhalb der üblichen Begrenzungen, ein Raum befindet, der jeden Moment schnell und einfach entfaltet werden kann, falls die Hauptstruktur verlängert werden muss. So öffnen sich auf geheimnisvolle Weise zwei Flügel, die das rechteckige Profil des Nomadenhauses zu einem offenen Fächer machen, der wie ein Pfau seine magischen Federn in einer Geste der Zurschaustellung zeigt. Für die Inszenierung der verschiedenen alltäglichen Abläufe ist der Wohnwagen in drei Zonen eingeteilt worden. So befinden sich Küche, Speisezimmer und Bad im Mittelteil, dem Herzstück des Wagens. Die beiden gelegentlich benutzten Bereiche werden zur Terrasse, wenn das gute Wetter dies möglich macht.

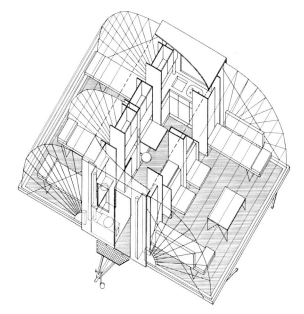

Axometry Axonométrie Axonometrische Ansicht

These two convertible spaces, screened off by lateral awnings concealed on each side of the main trunk, configure a sitting room within the transparent section.

Ces deux zones temporaires, couvertes de vélums latéraux, surgis des flancs du tronc principal, configurent le séjour dans la partie transparente.

Die beiden Bereiche, die nur gelegentlich benutzt und von seitlichen Markisen, gedeckt werden, bilden ein Wohnzimmer in dieser transparenten Sektion.

In good weather, the sitting room becomes a terrace.

Quand il fait beau, le séjour devient terrasse.

Wenn das Wetter gut ist, wird das Wohnzimmer zur Terrasse.

# Atelier in a Mountain
## Atelier de montagne
## Atelier in den Bergen

Toshihiko Suzuki

A dream location, where the imagination cannot conceive of building a permanent dwelling that covers the land and forever denies the flowering of its fruits. The ability to find a space in this imagined site in the middle of the mountains; a place to work, away from conventional offices, to be able to enjoy a cup of tea, to relax, to think. All these evocations were the starting point of the long process that marked this project, made real within parameters of mobility, flexibility, and maneuverability. A practical and ceremonial space was defined by two main units, one called shelter and the other air stream. Different mobile elements make up the first unit, which creates an atmosphere conducive to celebrate the tea ceremony. Complementing this small refuge is a type of trailer that acts as a preparatory room, a foretaste or substitute for the tea culture and its tradition.

Un lieu de rêve pour vivre, où l'on ne peut imaginer la construction d'une habitation permanente masquant la terre et la privant de ses fruits pour toujours. Pouvoir trouver un espace dans ce site imaginaire en pleine montagne : un lieu où travailler, loin des bureaux conventionnels, où prendre le thé, se relaxer et laisser libre cours à ses pensées. Toutes ces réflexions sont le point de départ de ce long cheminement à l'origine de ce projet, devenu réalité en suivant des paramètres comme la mobilité, la flexibilité et la maniabilité. Un espace pratique et cérémonial défini par deux unités principales, appelées « refuge » et « courant d'air ». La première des unités est composée d'éléments mobiles, créant l'ambiance propice pour célébrer la cérémonie du thé. Pour parachever ce petit refuge, il y a une sorte de caravane, à l'instar d'une antichambre, comme avant-goût ou substitut de la culture du thé et de ses traditions.

Ein traumhafter Ort zum Leben, an dem die Phantasie den Bau eines festen, beständigen Hauses, das die Erde verbirgt und ihre Früchte für immer zerstört, nicht wahr haben will. Ein Ort, wie man ihn nur erträumen kann, mitten in den Bergen, ein Ort zum Arbeiten, weit von den konventionellen Büros entfernt, oder ein Ort, um Tee zu trinken, sich zu entspannen und nachzudenken. Alle diese Gedanken waren der Ausgangspunkt für den unendlichen Weg, den diese Planung darstellte, und der zur Wirklichkeit wurde, in dem man den Parametern Mobilität, Flexibilität und Steuerbarkeit folgte. Ein praktischer und feierlicher Raum, der durch zwei Haupteinheiten definiert wird, die „Zufluchtsort" und „Luftstrom" genannt werden. Verschiedene mobile Elemente bilden die erste Einheit, in der die passende Umgebung für die Teezeremonie geschaffen wurde. Um diesen kleinen Zufluchtsort zu ergänzen, sieht man eine Art Karawane, die als Raum der Vorbereitung oder Ersatz für die Kultur des Tees und deren Tradition dient.

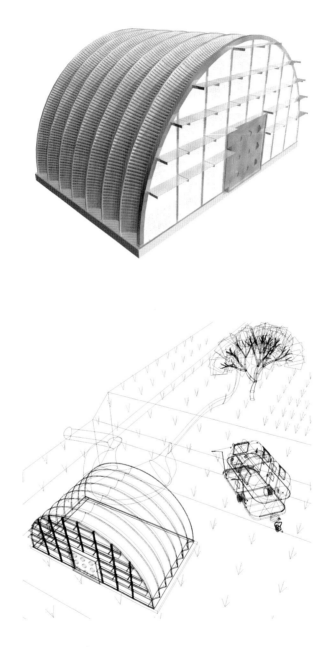

Axometries Axonométries Axonometrische Ansichten

The first of the units is formed of several movable elements that integrate fully with the surrounding landscape.

La première des unités est formée de différents éléments mobiles qui s'intègrent à l'atmosphère.

Die erste der Einheiten besteht aus verschiedenen, mobilen Elementen, die sich in die Umgebung integrieren.

This mountain refuge is an ideal spot for getting some work done, enjoying a cup of tea or simply relaxing.

Ce refuge situé au coeur de la montagne est le lieu idéal pour travailler, prendre un thé ou simplement se détendre.

Diese Hütte mitten in den Bergen ist der ideale Ort zum Arbeiten, Tee trinken oder einfach nur, um sich zu entspannen.

# ☐ **Ho & Ho**

Happy Living

Capsule shapes are cut into the walls to create interior spaces with a futuristic feeling, making the house look like a spaceship. These oval outlines in the walls serve the function of a door or a window, and at the same time they create a transition space for rest and relaxation. Passing from one room to another gives us the sense that we must pause or sit down to meditate, sigh, or just breathe. It all looks like an optical illusion, far from conventional domestic interiors; a fictional scene lit by neon lights and an illuminated sign with the word nostalgia, a melancholy reminder of a past that can be sensed in the utensils in the kitchen. The interior opens completely to the exterior and becomes integrated with nature, in an introverted attitude of subtle isolation and self-protection.

Les contours de capsules découpent les murs et définissent des intérieurs à l'ambiance futuriste, rapprochant l'habitation de l'image d'une navette spatiale. Ces silhouettes ovales qui partagent les murs en sections, encadrent une porte ou une fenêtre, tout en recherchant un espace de transition réservé à la détente et le repos. Aller d'une pièce à l'autre permet d'ouvrir les rideaux sur un entracte ou un murmure, incitant à s'asseoir pour méditer, soupirer ou tout simplement, respirer. Tout est illusion optique, loin de l'environnement domestique conventionnel : une scène de fiction sous un éclairage aux néons et des lettres lumineuses formant le mot nostalgie, souvenir mélancolique d'un passé que l'on devine au travers des ustensiles de cuisine. L'intérieur, entièrement ouvert sur l'extérieur, s'intègre à la nature, tout en gardant une attitude introvertie de doux isolement et d'autoprotection.

Umrisse von Kapseln zeichnen sich an den Wänden ab und definieren innere Bereiche mit futuristischem Charakter, die diese Wohnung einem Raumschiff gleichen lässt. Diese ovalen Profile, die die Wände unterteilen, dienen als Tür oder Fenster und versuchen gleichzeitig einen Raum des Übergangs für die Ruhe und Entspannung zu schaffen. Wenn man von einem Raum in den anderen gelangt, bereitet man sich darauf vor, sich hinzusetzen, um zu meditieren, zu seufzen oder einfach nur zu atmen. Das alles wird wie eine optische Illusion dargestellt, die weit von einer normalen Wohnumgebung entfernt ist. Eine fiktive Szenerie, die durch Neonlampen und Leuchtschilder mit dem Wort Sehnsucht erhellt wird. Eine melancholische Erinnerung an die Vergangenheit, die man zwischen den Küchenutensilien zu spüren glaubt. Das Innere öffnet sich vollständig nach außen und wird in die Natur integriert, wobei eine introvertierte Haltung und ein subtiler Selbstschutz und Isolation bewahrt werden.

Encapsulated spaces define futuristic areas within this interior space, creating a spaceship-like atmosphere in the home.

Des contours de capsules découpent les murs et définissent des intérieurs à l'ambiance futuriste, rapprochant l'habitation de l'image d'une navette spatiale.

Konturen mit Kapseln definieren die inneren Bereiche dieser futuristischen Umgebung und lassen die Wohnung wie ein Raumschiff aussehen.

The interior is fully open to the exterior and merges with its natural surroundings, preserving, nevertheless, a character of its own.

L'intérieur s'ouvre entièrement sur l'extérieur et s'intègre à la nature, tout en conservant son prope caractère.

Das Innere öffnet sich vollständig nach außen und integriert die Natur, ohne dabei seinen eigenen Charakter zu verlieren.

Photo credits Crédits photographiques Fotonachweis

p. 10-15        Douglas Fogelson

p. 16-23        Undine Pröhl

p. 24-29        Hélène Binet

p. 30-39        Eugeni Pons

p. 40-47        Jordi Miralles

p. 48-55        Bert Leandersson

p. 56-61        Juan Merinero

p. 62-67        Matteo Piazza

p. 68-73        Ángel Luis Baltanás

p. 74-79        Matteo Piazza

p. 80-85        Patrik Engquist

p. 86-91        Steve Schappacher, Rhea White

p. 92-97        Elisabeth Felicella

p. 98-103       Núria Fuentes

p. 104-109      Alan Williams

p. 110-115      Margherita Spiluttini

p. 116-121      Christian Richters

p. 122-127      Marc Mormeneo

p. 128-133      Hervé Abadie

p. 134-139      Ester Havlova

p. 140-145      Brett Boardman

p. 146-151      J.D. Peterson

p. 152-157      Tim Hursley

p. 158-163      Christian Richters

p. 164-169      Earl Carter / Taverne Agency

p. 170-175      Ross Aldershoff

p. 176-181      Toshihiko Suzuki

p. 182-189      Happy Living